# Contents

**Appendices**

The Department of National Heritage

# Library Information Series No. 21

# Schools Library Services and Financial Delegation to Schools

a report to the Department of National Heritage

by Coopers & Lybrand

July 1994

LONDON: HMSO

The Department of National Heritage
2–4 Cockspur Street
London
SW1Y 5DH
Switchboard: 071-211 6000

# Foreword

Almost all local authorities with education responsibilities in England and Wales provide a Schools Library Service. This need for adequate learning materials in schools, to promote pupils' learning and personal development, has been stressed by Her Majesty's Inspectorate of Schools for many years, and the introduction of the National Curriculum has strengthened this need. The Schools Library Service offers a cost-effective way for schools to provide the necessary range and quality of learning materials for both teachers and pupils.

At the same time, the introduction of Local Management of Schools, with the consequent delegation to individual schools of a high proportion of the budget related to school expenditure, has required local authorities to rethink the ways in which they finance, package and deliver their Schools Library Service. Many services have already re-established themselves as business units, or are moving in that direction. However, the considerable initial resource investment required for a Schools Library Service to operate in the first place, not only makes it more vulnerable to changes in demand than most other delegated services, but also means that it will only remain viable if most schools continue to subscribe to it. It is vital, therefore, that the service is managed, packaged and marketed to schools in the most effective ways, and that initial decisions on the allocation of delegated budgets do not disadvantage the service.

This report identifies and addresses the key issues relating to resource allocation and delegation; the marketing of services; and service structure and management which those responsible for providing or taking decisions relating to Schools Library Services need to address. It is intended to provide practical guidance to help ensure that schools, and the pupils and teachers within them, continue to have access to the learning resources they need. I commend it to Schools Library Service managers, chief librarians, chief education officers and councillors of local authorities.

**IAIN SPROAT**
**Parliamentary Under-Secretary of State**

# Summary of conclusions

**1**  Coopers and Lybrand were commissioned by the Department of National Heritage to review aspects of School Library Services (SLSs) in England and Wales in the light of the trend towards delegation of budgets to schools and in order to offer advice to managers and to local and national policy makers.

**2**  The review covered three main areas: resource allocation and delegation; the marketing of services; and structure and management issues.

## Resource allocation and delegation

**3**  There are operational features of SLSs which support partial delegation of budgets only and a higher proportion of central holdback than for other educational support services.

**4**  Devolution (or 'earmarking') of the SLS budget offers a 'halfway' house between central retention and delegation but is unlikely to offer a long-term alternative to delegation. It should only be introduced by Local Authorities (LAs) where schools are convinced of the benefits.

**5**  Resource allocation to schools needs to strike a balance between maintaining historical patterns of usage and encouraging newer patterns based on objective need. LAs should attempt to ensure that services are allocated on an equitable basis to schools within sectors prior to delegation. Formula arrangements should be designed to protect vulnerable users such as small schools.

**6**  Phasing of delegation by sector is appropriate for large SLSs but less so for small SLSs. A minimum of 12 months prior planning for delegation is sensible.

**7**  There is some evidence of increased use of the public library service by schools following delegation; this needs to be monitored more closely at a local and national level so that a fuller picture is obtained. Local SLSs and public library services should draw up a code of conduct setting out their respective roles and responsibilities and circulate it to staff and schools.

**8**  The budgets of SLSs need to be disentangled from other library budgets, even if the funds for shared support services are not delegated. This does not mean that the SLS and other library services need to operate as entirely separate services.

## Marketing and services

**9**  Charges for services are affected by the level of buy back by schools (normally less than 100%) and the full take up of service entitlement by those schools buying back. Charges should be set by reference to market conditions and not solely on the basis of costs. New services should generally be priced to at least cover full costs.

**10** Market definition for services is likely to become more school specific both between and within sectors. Market research techniques which involve working with representatives of schools are the most productive. Market research and promotional activities should be used as part of a continuous marketing process.

**11** Service packages are likely to become more individualised and flexible over time to meet school requirements but some schools may prefer to retain a more straightforward package approach. Flexible menu approaches can limit the scope for cross subsidy of services and affect stock requirements. Personal contact, albeit time consuming, is the most effective way of promoting services.

**12** The identification and promotion of new services is an emerging issue for SLSs. Successful approaches share the characteristic of working closely with users at the school level. There is also a need to develop a culture inside the SLS which encourages staff to innovate and improve performance.

**13** Service agreements should be clear, concise and specific. There would be advantages in allowing them to run for unspecified periods, provided schools have the freedom to terminate them at any time with adequate notice. Service agreements with grant maintained (GM) and independent schools need to be written as legally binding service contracts.

**14** Each SLS needs to investigate the buying process in its own locality to understand the roles of the key decision makers and target them effectively. Schools should be encouraged to adopt decision-making processes which are informed by the views of the teachers who use the service. They should also be encouraged to take their purchasing decisions in collaboration with other schools or at least in the knowledge of the decisions of other schools.

**15** Demonstrating 'value for money' to schools depends primarily on showing that services contribute to the raising of standards in schools and the meeting of schools' objectives. It also depends on demonstrating that services are less costly than other alternatives (such as book purchase) and on ensuring that service standards are met consistently.

**16** There is no evidence to suggest that a commercial provider of loan services will emerge if SLSs decline. A general decline could impact on the range and quality of learning materials in schools and, through this, on the effective delivery of the National Curriculum. It might also impact on children's publishing generally and lead to a narrower range of material being published by commercial publishers.

**17** SLSs should emphasise their professional skills and independence in the provision of book purchase advice and consultancy and training. Competition between different service units within an LA for the provision of similar services to schools should be avoided.

**18** The possible restrictions on trading with GM schools in the long term could impact seriously on the viability of some SLSs. The advice and guidance on this promised by the Department for Education (DFE) should be of value. Restrictions on cross-border trading are less immediate but could have a similar effect of locking SLSs into a declining 'home' market; they could also prevent schools having access to an alternative provider in cases where their own LA's service declines.

## Structure and management

**19**  LAs need to establish a coherent framework for their in-house trading units. Decisions on strategic issues relating to service delivery should require agreement by the LA but SLS managers should have the same operational flexibility as LMS schools.

**20**  Improved management information and systems are required by many SLSs. Managers should draw up a list of their requirements and ascertain whether these are available through in-house developments. Non-delegated SLSs should carry out this exercise prior to delegation.

**21**  SLSs should be full cost centres with a trading account for income and expenditure purposes. Business plans require at least six months to develop and should project more than one year ahead.

**22**  SLSs require a range of new business skills to operate effectively in a trading environment but this need not undermine the professional leadership of the service. LAs should identify and make provision to meet the new training needs. The strong customer orientation of SLSs makes them better placed to manage the transition to trading than many other services.

**23**  Close links and collaboration between the SLS and other educational trading services are productive. This may weaken the historical linkage with the public library services but not in all LAs. Central support service costs are likely to become increasingly under the control of trading units.

**24**  The prospect of SLSs being 'externalised' from LAs is not welcomed by SLS managers generally but many view it as inevitable to overcome trading restrictions and as a consequence of local government reorganisation. Few have investigated the various options yet.

**25**  Local government reorganisation is likely to have a major impact on SLSs in County areas with possible losses of scale, expertise and breadth of service if fragmentation occurs. There are alternatives to fragmentation but all have potential disadvantages too. SLSs with experience of delegation and trading are more likely to survive the changes brought about by reorganisation.

# I Introduction

**101**  Coopers & Lybrand were commissioned by the Department of National Heritage (DNH) to carry out a review of Schools Library Services (SLSs) in England and Wales in the light of the general movement towards delegation of budgets to schools. The review therefore focused on the experience of delegation and the changes that had occurred rather than all aspects of SLSs.

## Background to the review

**102**  Almost all local authorities[1] (LAs) with education responsibilities in England and Wales provide an SLS. The range of services provided by each typically includes loans of books and project materials, and advice on book purchase and the maintenance and development of libraries within schools.

**103**  The need for adequate learning materials in schools to promote pupils' learning and personal development has been underlined by Her Majesty's Inspectors (HMI) for many years. The introduction of the National Curriculum strengthens this need and the new inspection framework for schools produced by the Office for Standards in Education (OFSTED) specifically includes inspection of resources for learning. It is within this context that the SLS can offer a cost-effective way for schools to provide the range and quality of learning materials which are necessary for teachers and pupils.

**104**  Following the 1988 Education Reform Act, the introduction of Local Management of Schools (LMS) obliged LAs to delegate to schools a high proportion of the budgets related to school expenditure. This included not only the budgets most closely associated with the direct running costs of schools (eg teachers' salaries, heating and lighting) but also the budgets for certain educational support services.

**105**  Although LAs have discretion over whether or not to delegate the budgets for individual educational support services (and, if so, what proportion of the budgets), this freedom is heavily circumscribed by the requirement to meet percentage targets set for delegation by the Department For Education (DFE). These targets have been increased over time such that, although only around half all LAs have delegated the budget for their SLS to date, a clear majority can be expected to do so.

**106**  The most recent picture of the extent of delegation by LAs is shown in *Table 1* overleaf which illustrates the extent of delegation in 1992/93 and that planned for 1994/95. The written submissions we received confirmed the general movement to delegation, and its acceleration in some cases.

---

[1] Throughout this report we use the term local authority (LA) to describe authorities with education responsibilities (ie counties, metropolitan districts and London boroughs). We do not use the term local education authority (LEA) as this is sometimes used to denote only services within the responsibility of the Education Committee or Education Department, which is rarely the case for the SLS and the public library service.

*Table 1:* **Extent of delegation of SLS by type of LA**

| | Actual by 1992/93 | | Planned by 1994/95 | | Total SLSs responding |
| --- | --- | --- | --- | --- | --- |
| | Primary Schools | Secondary Schools | Primary Schools | Secondary Schools | |
| English Counties | 5 | 11 | 20 | 26 | 38 |
| Metropolitan Districts | 2 | 2 | 11 | 11 | 35 |
| Inner London | 4 | 3 | 6 | 4 | 9 |
| Outer London | 3 | 4 | 11 | 10 | 19 |
| Wales | 1 | 0 | 4 | 3 | 8 |
| **Total** | **15** | **20** | **52** | **54** | **109** |

Source: *A Survey of Library Services to Schools and Children in the UK 1992/93* – Library and Information Statistics Unit, Loughborough University of Technology, 1993.

## Terms of reference

**107**    The main aim of the review was to investigate the experience of delegation and to identify the lessons that could be learnt. Three key areas were identified for investigation:

– **resource allocation and delegation** – including the advantages and disadvantages of delegation, devolution, the allocation of delegated resources to schools, the timing and phasing of delegation, the impact of delegation on public library services, and the disentangling of budgets;

– **marketing of services** – including the relationship between costs and charges, market definition and market research, service definition and promotion, new services, service agreements, roles in the buying process, value for money, competition, and trading barriers;

– **structure and management** – including the managerial freedoms required by some managers, management information and systems, trading structures and business planning, new business skills, relationships with other parts of the LA, externalisation, and the implications of local government reorganisation.

**108**    The remaining sections of this report mirror these key areas. The full list of issues explored for each is included in *Appendix A*.

**109**    The review should be of value to three separate audiences:

– **managers of SLSs** preparing for delegation, or already running services under delegation, by providing them with practical guidance and advice;

– **decision makers within LAs**, by providing advice on the particular characteristics of SLSs which need to be taken into account when considering the introduction or further development of delegation schemes.

– **national policy makers**, by identifying any dangers to the long-term success of SLSs which arise from delegation or other changes.

## Approach

**110**    The fieldwork for the review was carried out through a request to all SLSs for written submissions and through visits to a small sample of SLSs as case studies.

**111**    The invitation to provide **written submissions** was despatched on 10 February 1994 to all SLS managers in England and Wales with a deadline of 11 March 1994 (copies were sent for information to the Head of the Public Library Service and the Chief Education Officer). Responses were received from 70 SLSs and from several national and umbrella bodies to which the invitation was sent for information. Several publishers and publishing organisations also provided information. A list of all those who responded is attached as *Appendix B.*

**112**    The **case studies** visited were Cheshire, Devon, Hillingdon, Kirklees, Lincolnshire and Sandwell. During each visit, interviews were held with the manager of the SLS, the head (or a senior manager) of the public library service, education officers responsible for the LMS scheme (and wider aspects of delegation) and head teachers. Some of the main characteristics of each case study SLS are summarised in *Appendix C.*

**113**    The review was overseen by a steering committee convened by the DNH and consisting of representatives of the DNH, the DFE, the OFSTED, the British Library and managers of SLSs. The membership of this steering committee and the consultancy team is given in *Appendix D.* We are grateful for the valuable comments provided by members of the Steering Committee during the review. However, the views expressed in the report are those of Coopers & Lybrand and not of the steering committee.

**114**    We are also grateful to all the SLSs and other organisations who provided written submissions and, in particular, to the six SLSs and their LAs that were willing to act as case studies.

# II   Resource allocation and delegation

## Introduction

**201**   In this section we consider resource allocation issues. These include the general advantages and disadvantages of delegation; the use of devolution rather than delegation; the allocation of resources to schools for delegated services; the timing and phasing of delegation; the impact of delegation on public library services; and the disentangling of budgets. For each issue we consider the findings from our fieldwork and the conclusions that we draw.

## Advantages and disadvantages of delegation

**202**   In those LAs which have decided to delegate the budget for the SLS the debate concerning the advantages and disadvantages of delegation is unlikely to be re-opened. However, in those which have yet to do so the experience of others will be more relevant.

### Findings

**203**   Nearly all written submissions devoted considerable space to this issue.
The most common **advantages** of delegation cited were:

— greater incentive to review service delivery, costs and management;

— more opportunities to respond to customer needs;

— greater protection from central budget cuts by the LA.

**204**   However, most submissions emphasised the **disadvantages** of budget delegation as compared with central funding. This was particularly true of submissions from SLSs which are currently funded centrally by their LAs. The most common disadvantages identified were:

— less security and continuity for the service;

— greater difficulty in strategic and operational planning;

— loss of economies of scale and greater difficulty in offering a wide and high quality range of services;

— more unequal access to services and a narrower customer base;

— complexity in sustaining services to customers without delegated budgets (eg nursery schools, pre-school playgroups, special needs units);

— undermining of the educational ethos of service delivery.

**205**   The position on delegation for the six case study SLSs is shown in *Appendix C*. Only three have their budgets delegated both to primary and to secondary schools, and all of these have some level of central hold back by the LA (varying between 8% and 50% of the budget) to cover central overheads. In several cases delegation had taken place in order to meet the DFE targets, or the general philosophy of the LA, and did not therefore necessarily reflect the preferences of the SLS or the expressed wishes of schools.

**206**   The advantages and disadvantages of delegation cited by SLS managers in the case studies were similar to those raised in the written submissions, although managers of delegated services placed more emphasis on the advantage of greater protection from central budget cuts by the LA. Likewise, these managers confirmed that the benefits of increased responsiveness to schools and greater efficiency had occurred following delegation.

**207**   Headteachers' views in the case study LAs were similar to those we have found elsewhere for other educational support services – no great enthusiasm for budget delegation at the outset but a welcome for the greater choice and freedom once it had been introduced. Some headteachers confirmed that whilst they currently give the service a high priority, this could not be guaranteed against other priorities in the future.

### Conclusions

**208**   In our view, there should be a general presumption in favour of delegating the budgets of educational support services to schools unless strong arguments can be marshalled to the contrary. For the SLS we think there are two possible counter-arguments to delegation: the first relates to the role of the client; the second to operational features.

**209**   In terms of the **role of the client,** there is agreement that the ultimate user (and thus client) of the SLS is the individual pupil. However, given that pupils are seldom involved in decisions about the range and volume of services to be made available to them, the debate is over who is best placed to make these decisions on their behalf; the LA or the school? By holding the budget centrally the LA is, in effect, arguing that it is better placed than the individual school to make this judgement and to balance this decision against other possible uses of the resources involved.

**210**   This is a valid position for an LA to take. However, the general philosophy of the LMS, which we support, is that the school is best placed to make decisions on educational support services for its pupils. We therefore find it difficult to oppose delegation of the budget for the SLS on these grounds.

**211**   In terms of **operational features** the argument against delegation relates to the fact that the SLS requires a considerable investment in resources to operate in the first place (in economic terms, it has a high ratio of fixed costs to variable costs). This makes it more vulnerable to changes in demand than most other delegated services and means that it requires a relatively high level of buy back from schools to operate at all.

**212**   We accept the logic of this operational argument but are not convinced that it is sufficiently strong to prevent delegation of any part of the SLS budget. Instead, it supports the central retention of a higher proportion of the budget by the LA than for other education support services. We therefore think that a model of partial delegation may be the most sensible strategy for LAs considering this issue.

## Delegation or devolution?

**Findings**

**213**   Faced with the difficulty of balancing the arguments in favour and against delegation, a small number of LAs (including one of the case studies) 'devolves' rather than delegates the budget for the SLS to schools. This approach seeks to give schools greater choice over the precise use of the budget without giving them the complete freedom to use the funds for any alternative priority. As such, it is similar to the earmarking arrangements used by the DFE for some of its grants for education support and training (GEST).

**214**   In the particular case study where this approach was used, the SLS budget was one of a number of budgets for learning support services devolved to schools. Within the total sum received by schools for these services, each school was free to buy more or less of any of the individual learning support services and to purchase the services from other providers, but it was not free to use the resources for other purposes (eg to appoint teaching staff). Thus the school is allowed to trade off priorities within a narrow range of services, all of which have a common theme (ie learning support).

**215**   Local managers saw this approach as a valuable 'half-way house' for the SLS, introducing a degree of market pressure whilst protecting the SLS from the full impact of free choice by schools. It underpinned the relatively high levels of buy back from schools that this SLS had achieved and appeared to be popular with many schools.

**Conclusions**

**216**   For some LAs, devolution may offer an attractive compromise between delegation and central retention. It can also be varied to allow different levels of freedom to schools depending on local circumstances (eg in terms of the choice of services between which funds can be vired, and whether providers other than the LA can be used). However, the devolved funds are still regarded by the DFE as part of the LA's centrally retained budget; they do not therefore count towards meeting the delegation targets set by the DFE.

**217**   It is also worth noting that devolution can only operate between LAs and LM schools, as it is not possible to earmark the funding of GM schools in the same way. This means it is unlikely to be a viable alternative in areas with large GM sectors.

**218**   In our view, devolution is unlikely to offer a long-term alternative to delegation, as the pressure for schools to exert greater control over their budgets is likely to strengthen rather than weaken over time. However, it may allow a breathing space during which SLSs can enter into a prolonged dialogue with schools and recast their services to meet schools' needs. It can also allow time for schools to become used to paying for library services and assessing value for money.

**219**   We therefore think that devolution is likely to form part of a slow phasing towards delegation, rather than to constitute an end in itself – a view shared by some of the LA managers in the case study which operated devolution. We also think that it should only be used where schools are convinced of the benefits and consent to its introduction in place of a more rapid move to delegation; this should not be a decision determined by the LA without consultation with its schools.

## Methods of allocating delegated resources to schools

**220**    Just as LAs are free to decide whether or not to delegate the SLS, they are also free to choose the most appropriate method of allocating the delegated resources to schools through the LMS formula. However, there are DFE targets for the proportion of the total resources delegated which must be allocated on the basis of pupil numbers; this can influence the method chosen by LAs for allocating delegated resources to schools for individual support services such as the SLS.

### Findings

**221**    From the written submissions, most LAs appear to have used a mixture of a lump sum and an amount per pupil to delegate the resources which had hitherto been spent on the SLS (less any central holdback). The lump sum acted as a protection for small schools and also reflected the argument that all schools need a minimum base of learning materials to deliver the National Curriculum.

**222**    Most LAs appear to have recognised the need to separate out the allocation for the primary sector from that for the secondary sector prior to delegation. There are, however, numerous examples where different approaches have been used, sometimes to the subsequent detriment of the SLS. A small number of LAs appears to have included a weighting for social deprivation on the pupil number element.

**223**    The ability of schools to see the amount which had been delegated to them notionally for the SLS appears to have been an issue in some LAs, particularly where delegation took place as part of a block with other services. Schools tend to compare the amount notionally delegated for the SLS with the charges set for the service (charges are considered more fully in *Section III*).

**224**    The case studies illustrated a range of allocation practices, including:

– by lump sum;

– by lump sum, per pupil and per pupil on free school meals;

– per pupil through the age weighted pupil unit (AWPU).

**225**    The use of AWPUs is a particular case in point as the heavier age weightings given to older pupils skew funding towards the secondary sector and away from the primary sector (which in most LAs has traditionally been the main user of the service).

### Conclusions

**226**    The way in which resources are allocated to schools is a critical influence on whether they are likely to buy back services. For many LAs, it will also raise questions of equity as most educational support services, including the SLS, will not have been delivered evenly across schools, either between or within sectors. There is therefore often a balance to be struck between maintaining historical patterns of usage, as far as this is possible, and allocating resources on a more equitable basis.

**227**    There is also a need to consider resource allocation and charges for services as part of a total policy for delegation because schools will look to make the link between the two when they make their initial purchasing decisions. This is most likely to influence them in the early years of delegation when the connection between the notional sums delegated and charges will be uppermost in school minds. However, schools should be encouraged to think in terms of the whole school budget rather than any notional allocations; the philosophy of the LMS is, of course, entirely opposed to the concept of schools being given particular allocations for particular services.

**228** We suggest that decisions on resource allocation might take place via the following steps:

– identify the different services which are to be delegated;
– identify the total costs of the different services which are to be delegated;
– decide the proportion of total costs which is to be delegated (the distinction between fixed and variable costs may be useful here);
– identify the use of these services by the relevant sectors (eg nursery, primary, secondary, special) and calculate the amounts that should go to each sector to maintain the historical position;
– decide whether the historical position is defensible on the basis of objective need. If not, consider re-allocating the service **prior** to delegation on a more equitable basis (this relates to service use within sectors too);
– test out different formula arrangements to achieve the desired individual allocations to schools (eg through different amounts for lump sums and per pupil factors, with or without weightings for social need);
– consider charges for services, particularly in the light of likely buy-back levels below 100%.

## Timing and phasing arrangements

**229** A feature of the approach of many LAs to the LMS is the gradual phasing in of services to delegation. This can apply to some or all educational support services and can take a variety of forms.

**Findings**
**230** The strong view from the written submissions is of the benefits of a cautious approach to delegation of the SLS, with adequate time for pre-planning. At least 12 months' notice of delegation is common and, even then, some SLS managers would prefer the first year to be used for earmarked (or devolved) funding rather than delegation.

**231** Various types of phasing have been used:

– by sector (usually secondary first, followed by primary, and then by special – although linking primary and special together is also common);

– by percentage of expenditure (eg 50% of expenditure in the first year and the full amount later), sometimes linked to increasing the range of SLS services to which delegation applies over the same period of time;

– by geographical area (eg one area of a County first, usually as a subset of phasing by sector and sometimes as a pilot).

**232**   Only phasing by sector is seen as successful, and even then a minority of SLSs (usually small metropolitan services) feels it overcomplicates matters. The disadvantage of phasing by percentage of expenditure is the shock for schools of steep price rises beyond the first year. Phasing by geographical area is only seen as appropriate in large Counties.

**233**   The case studies reflected the range of views expressed in the written submissions although several, from personal experience, endorsed a 'big bang' approach to delegation which avoided phasing altogether (this was very much with hindsight however; there was concern about the absence of phasing at the time). The use of the planning period for market research, cost centre establishment, training and development of service agreements was emphasised.

### Conclusions

**234**   We think that a minimum of 12 months' prior planning for delegation is sensible. We also support phasing by sector for large SLSs, but think it less appropriate for small SLSs unless the ability to use the experience in one sector to fine tune the approach for another is likely to outweigh the disadvantage of having to run dual systems during the transition period.

## Impact on public library services

### Findings

**235**   The possible impact of a decline in the use by schools of SLSs on public library services was a major concern of the DNH and a prime factor behind the commissioning of this review. The potential implications for the public library service are two-fold:

- an increase in the use by schools of what they perceive to be the 'free' public library service as an alternative to the paid SLS;

- a decline in shared support services if the SLS can no longer meet its contribution from the income it wins back from schools.

### Findings

**236**   The possibility of schools looking to the **'free' public library service** as an alternative to the SLS was raised in all written submissions and case study visits. The public library service was generally seen as already under pressure to provide support to pupils outside of school hours. This pressure had risen since the introduction of the National Curriculum and many SLSs doubted the ability of public libraries to respond further than they do at present.

**237**   Several submissions gave examples of teachers from schools which had not subscribed to the SLS making greater use of public library services and also organising more frequent class visits to public libraries for their pupils. This appears to be a growing phenomenon although we are not aware of any national statistical evidence which identifies its true scale.

**238**  Possible local strategies put forward by SLS managers to prevent this occurring included:

— withdrawal of teacher tickets and special lending rights where these exist (some public library services have already taken this step);

— restrictions on adults borrowing more than a small number of children's non-fiction books;

— restrictions on class visits to libraries;

— clarification of the respective roles and responsibilities of the public library service and the SLS and formalisation of them into a code of conduct which is circulated to all library staff and to schools;

— maintenance of special access rights (eg teacher tickets, regular class visits, library staff visits to schools) only to schools subscribing to the SLS;

— charging for services from public libraries which can be deemed to be for the school rather than for individuals (although it was accepted that the distinction between the two could be difficult to establish and some thought this strategy unworkable in practice);

— a radical recasting of the two services (either for all schools or just for secondary schools) so that, in future, the SLS was offered through local branches of public libraries by public library service staff, drawing upon specialist support from SLS staff when necessary.

**239**  In terms of **shared support services** the experience of SLS managers varied widely depending on the level of integration between the SLS and public library service and the existence of service agreements between the two. Thus for some managers the knock-on effect on the public library service of the potential decline (or expansion) of the SLS as a result of delegation was seen as minimal; for others it was a major issue. The main problems in integrated services appeared to relate to shared stock and shared bibliographical and IT systems.

**Conclusions**

**240**  Although the evidence is largely anecdotal at this stage, it is clear that the impact of delegation on the public library service could be considerable if delegation leads to an increase in use by schools (as the evidence suggests). We think that public library services and SLSs should jointly monitor changes in demand so that a fuller picture can be established. At a national level, the DNH and the DFE (the latter possibly via OFSTED inspections) should look to co-ordinate and augment this local effort in order to build up a national picture.

**241**  Of the various possible future strategies identified, we think the clarification of the respective roles and responsibilities of the public library service and the SLS is a vital first step. This will allow the creation of a code of conduct which can be agreed by staff and circulated to schools. Subsequent measures to restrict the rights of teachers and pupils to use public library services other than as individuals should only be contemplated when this step has failed to resolve the issue and when reliable evidence of planned and excessive school use of the public library service is available.

**242**   The problems of shared support systems for some SLSs are real but not, in our view, insuperable given that some services appear to have resolved the potential difficulties through service agreements and revised accountancy procedures.

# Disentangling of budgets

**243**   Delegation of budgets to schools has required more precise costing of services and definition of budgets than was hitherto the case in LAs. The exercise can be more difficult for services which are integrated with other services in terms of delivery and support functions; this is true of many SLSs with respect to the public library service.

## Findings

**244**   The written submissions suggested that the disentangling of the SLS budget from the budgets for other library services was a time-consuming but relatively straightforward exercise in many LAs. Book funds were normally held as a discrete item and so caused few problems; staffing and overheads were less clear cut. For staffing, shared professional and administration posts sometimes required a diary exercise to calculate the correct division. Overheads were the greatest problem and were usually apportioned by using proxies for their use (eg by staff numbers, or by floorspace in the case of premises costs).

**245**   The funding of vehicles was also an issue in several LAs. This related less to running costs and more to the extent to which the SLS was expected to make a contribution to replacement costs.

**246**   The case studies allowed us to pursue some of these issues further. In one an exercise to establish the SLS as a separate cost centre prior to delegation had defined budgets at a very detailed level such that clear breakdowns were available for all the various types of overhead. This had proved valuable to the later planning for delegation, although the decision not to delegate more than 50% of the budget meant that this level of detail was not critical. In another case study the problem had been avoided by retaining all shared costs centrally and continuing with notional budget distinctions.

## Conclusions

**247**   We think it important to disentangle the budget of the SLS from other budgets as part of the planning for delegation, although this is less crucial in the early stages if the budgets for shared activities are not delegated. However, even where these elements are held centrally (which we think sensible) they will need to be calculated in due course if SLS managers are to have full managerial freedom over their services (and the support costs they carry). There is also another reason to disentangle these costs and that is to show central administrative costs accurately in the LA's Section 42 statement which, for some LAs, is used to calculate central service budget entitlements for local GM schools.

**248**   It is also important to be clear on the responsibilities within the LA for replacement of equipment and vehicles, and for minor capital expenditure. This will allow the SLS to budget for any responsibilities it has in these areas.

**249**   We suspect that one of the less tangible barriers to unravelling the budgets of shared support services may relate to a reluctance to see the SLS and the public library service operate as two entirely separate services. We understand this reluctance but would emphasise that budget separation need not lead to operational separation. Thus the traditional close working and support between the services can be maintained where these are valued highly. One SLS manager described this as a 'velcro' join between the two services; a strong link that can be separated easily when required for financial or other reasons.

# III  Marketing of services

## Introduction

**301**  In this section we consider the ways in which services are marketed to schools by SLSs. This includes the relationship between: costs and charges; market definition and market research; service definition and promotion; new services; service agreements; roles in the buying process; value for money; competition; and barriers to trading.

## Costs and charges

**302**  The relationship between the costs of providing services to schools and the charges made for them is complicated by a number of factors. These include the need to estimate the likely level of buy back by schools and the need to decide whether some services should be used to cross subsidise others. There is also the question of whether services should aim to make a surplus or not.

### Findings

**303**  Most delegated SLSs appear to have operated a cost or 'cost plus' approach to charges, once the level of central hold back (or subsidy) is taken into account. For example, in the case study which delegates 50% of the budget, charges need only to recoup half of the services' costs. 'Cost plus' is usually interpreted as the need to make a small surplus to cover future developments and promotional activities.

**304**  The major difficulty in setting charges has been the unpredictability of buy back by schools. Some SLSs were required by their LAs to assume a full buy back and thus made a loss in the first year; others assumed a certain 'opt out' rate and set their charges accordingly (some LAs set a guideline rate for this, such as a 5% uprating of charges). One SLS included in its service agreement with schools a promise to consult with them on the use of any surpluses made.

**305**  Where schools have failed to buy back to the anticipated level, many SLSs have felt unable to raise charges to the subscribing schools for fear of further schools not buying back. This has led SLSs to look for efficiency improvements first and then service reductions to offset the income reductions faced. However, the limited scope for efficiency improvements to achieve dramatic savings has meant that service and staff reductions have often followed delegation.

**306**  As delegation develops SLSs have began to look at more 'market driven' approaches to pricing, in which considerations of what the market will bear and the level of competition figure alongside cost considerations. Some are willing to subsidise certain services (eg advisory support) because they see them as useful promotional opportunities for services in general.

**307**  No SLS appears to be distinguishing its charges to schools on the basis of the differential costs of serving certain types of schools (eg charging remote rural schools more than urban schools because of extra travel time). SLS managers in the case studies doubted whether their LAs would allow such an approach as schools are not funded differentially to take account of these factors; nor did they wish to see this development themselves.

**308**   Charges to GM and independent schools were generally higher to reflect the lack of LA hold back or subsidy. There was no evidence of SLSs looking to make additional surpluses from these sectors to subsidise other activities.

**Conclusions**

**309**   We think that 'cost plus' is a realistic form of pricing for SLSs in the early years of delegation when SLSs are seeking to establish themselves on a trading basis and schools are becoming familiar with operating in a market. Thereafter, more 'market driven' pricing can be developed which is sensitive to school priorities and competitive pressures.

**310**   Showing individual schools the sum delegated to them (ie their share of the sum previously spent centrally by the LA on the SLS) can help to reassure them that provision has been made in their budgets. However, this is against the philosophy of the LMS which does not encourage notional allocations for particular services. It can also lead to difficulties as charges for the historical level of service may well need to be higher than the amount notionally delegated to the individual school. There are two main reason for this:

− less than full buy back by schools means that the shortfall in income will need to be recouped in part from higher charges to subscribing schools;

− a more even take up of service entitlement by schools across the LA results in greater demands on the SLS and a consequent need to increase charges (to fund an expansion of services) or to decrease service levels to those schools previously favoured. This experience is common for many services moving from a 'free' to a paid basis (ie customers require their full entitlement when they are footing the bill).

**311**   Although the central overheads of many SLSs are met by centrally retained funds, new or additional services should be priced to (at least) cover their full costs (ie not share in the central subsidy too) unless there are good developmental or promotional reasons for doing otherwise.

## Market definition and market research

**312**   The movement to a trading basis has required SLSs to define the customers for their services more precisely. It has also required them to seek customer views on a more systematic basis through market research.

**Findings**

**313**   Most SLSs define their markets primarily in terms of the different sectors of LA schools (primary, secondary, special). GM and independent schools are seen as separate markets, as are the internal customers within the LA (eg the Advisory Service). Some SLSs have now moved to a more detailed breakdown of customers and markets within these sectors (eg heads of department within secondary schools, subject teachers and language co-ordinators).

**314**   Most delegated SLSs carried out specific market research with schools prior to delegation to assist them in defining their service offer. This often included postal questionnaires, telephone interviews, attendance at headteachers' meetings and use of 'customer forums'. The target of this research was predominantly headteachers but sometimes included teachers and governors.

**315**   Research techniques which involve personal contact (eg customer forums) appear to have proved more valuable than questionnaires. This was confirmed by headteachers in the case study visits who preferred personal contact with service providers.

**316**   Collaboration with other trading units within the LA which provide services to schools has proved valuable for some SLSs, particularly in terms of sharing market research exercises. This is often co-ordinated by the LA to prevent schools being bombarded with separate requests.

**Conclusions**

**317**   Market definition is likely to become more specific, both between and within schools as they become more differentiated in their buying patterns. Some schools may emerge as 'service leaders' and be particularly important to monitor because of their receptiveness to the development of new services and their role in influencing other schools.

**318**   Market research techniques which involve working with schools to define new markets and services are likely to be more productive than generalised surveys. However, this is time consuming and it is unlikely to be feasible to include all schools (the need for those included to be representative therefore arises).

**319**   Market research and promotional activities should not be seen as separate undertakings; they are both part of the marketing process. Likewise, market research is a continuous activity and not a one-off exercise.

## Service definition and promotion

**320**   Closely allied to market definition and market research is the definition of the services to be offered and their promotion to schools. This has been a new area for many educational support services.

**Findings**

**321**   SLSs have developed a wide variety of **service definitions** of their 'offer' but the main types can be summarised as follows:

– a single 'take-it-or-leave-it' package at a fixed package price, sometimes with optional add-ons at extra charges. The package can include all the services previously offered or it can be a basic package (consisting of, say, the book loan service and a limited amount of advisory work) with optional add-ons at extra charges;

– a variable package at a fixed package price, within which schools are able to opt for different services and different service levels;

- a variable package at a variable package price, within which schools choose different levels and are charged different prices;

- a set of modules (or sub-packages) of services which schools use to assemble a particular package. Modules are individually priced and schools often receive a discount for purchasing more than one;

- an open menu of services from which schools construct an individual customised package. Each service is individually priced and discounts for bulk purchases may be available.

**322**  Many SLSs started out with a 'take-it-or-leave-it' package and are now working their way progressively through more flexible offers. The demand for and pace of this is faster with secondary schools than with primary schools.

**323**  Within any of these approaches charges can be set per package (or service), or per pupil, or by some combinations of the two (eg a minimum subscription plus a per pupil fee above the minimum). Often an attempt is made to match the format of the charge to the way in which funds are delegated (eg lump sum and/or per pupil). 'Pay as you use' for an open menu of services is offered as an alternative to packages by some SLSs, usually at a higher charge than an equivalent package.

**324**  SLSs have used a variety of **promotional methods** for informing schools of the service offer. These include:

- inclusion of details in the LA's brochure of services alongside other offers from trading units;

- separate written material, such as brochures and letters to headteachers, governors and teachers, and regular newsletters. However, some SLSs consciously avoided this, following advice from schools that additional publicity was seen as wasteful of resources, particularly if it involved 'glossy' leaflets;

- detailed information for individual schools listing the precise extent of their previous use of the service (say, over the last 12 months);

- 'open days' for potential customers to visit services — either as part of LA organised 'trade fairs' for services or as separate events;

- attendance at headteachers' meetings and governors' forums to present details of the service offer and answer questions;

- visits to individual schools to discuss details with the headteacher and staff.

**325**  Personal contact between professional staff and customers is seen as the most effective means of providing information and promoting services. However, as noted earlier for market research, this is time consuming for SLS staff and for schools. One case study SLS makes it a policy never to ask for more than 30 minutes of a headteacher's time during a school visit unless a longer period is sought by the school.

**Conclusions**

**326**  SLSs are likely to need to offer more flexible packages of services over time to allow schools more individualised choices, particularly secondary schools. But the pace of this development needs to be agreed with customers as some schools, or sectors, may prefer to remain with a more straightforward subscription based package. SLSs should not ignore the wishes of these schools to retain a simpler approach. They should also ensure that the complexity of the service packages on offer are not off-putting.

**327**   Flexible menu approaches generally offer less scope for the cross-subsidy of services than more comprehensive packages. They can also have an effect on stock requirements by SLSs. In general they are likely to require a greater range and depth of stock; this may impact on charges for services.

**328**   Personal contact is the most effective way of informing schools of the service offer and of promoting services. But, once again, this needs to be sensitive to the wishes of schools, some of which resent promotional activities that consume resources and school time. The length of time spent with customers is likely to be less important than the quality of that time.

# New services

**329**   Although the experience of delegation has often resulted in service reductions as a result of a less than 100% buy back from schools, some SLSs have managed to develop and promote new services. This is likely to become a more important activity over time and to be a vital aspect in maintaining a successful SLS in the long term.

**Findings**

**330**   Of those SLSs which have been proactive and managed to **identify new services** since delegation, the following techniques appear to be most common:

- ideas generation by SLS staff through SWOT (strengths – weaknesses – opportunities – threats) analysis and brainstorming;

- analysis of customer surveys and other feedback (eg complaints, suggestion slips on project loan boxes);

- interviews and discussions with headteachers and teachers, often through small representative 'customer forums';

- liaison with the LA's Advisory Service on curriculum developments;

- reviews of developments elsewhere by library services and by other educational trading services.

**331**   Identification and development of ideas with small representative groups of customers appears to have been the most successful approach. Although we did not ask for specific examples of new services or service variations as part of the review, a list of some of the examples most commonly highlighted to us is included as *Appendix E.*

**332**   **Promotion of new services** to schools has also involved a variety of approaches:

- special publicity mailings to schools, in letter or leaflet form, and publicity in regular newsletters (although some SLSs see regular newsletters as unnecessary, unless there is something substantive to say in each edition);

- school visits and demonstrations, preferably as part of a wider exercise to review services;

- 'guest spots' at conferences, meetings and, in particular, INSET courses;

- pilots with committed schools to test out benefits and demonstrate value to other schools;

- special events such as 'open days', quizzes, writing and art competitions, and visits by children's authors;

- special introductory offers at below full price;

- sponsorship from publishers and library suppliers.

## Conclusions

**333**  The identification and promotion of new services is a valuable activity for all SLSs. Although a variety of approaches have emerged the common characteristic is an emphasis on working closely with customers. This is likely to involve users at the classroom level (eg class teachers and, through them, pupils) as well as headteachers.

**334**  SLSs should also take steps to create a culture which encourages all staff to participate in the identification of new services and improvement of existing services. This is consistent with the general trend in the public and private service sectors towards devolving greater responsibility to staff for innovation and performance improvement (eg through the various quality initiatives such as BS5750/ISO8000, Total Quality Management and Investors in People).

## Service agreements

**335**  The normal means of making delegated services available to schools is through a formal service agreement setting out the range and frequency of services to be provided, the charges and the conditions of service delivery. The types of service packages offered by SLSs were described earlier; here we discuss the general characteristics of service agreements and the extent to which they balance the needs of schools against the needs of SLSs for future viability.

### Findings

**336**  There was consensus that schools and SLSs derived mutual benefits from having formal service agreements which were concise, clear and specific. There was less consensus, however, on whether service agreements were statements of intentions (to be met if at all possible) or guarantees of service delivery (to be penalised if not met). Several SLSs commented that schools saw them as guarantees and that it was therefore vital to ensure that they did not include over-optimistic targets (or, alternatively, that they clearly stated that the SLS could not guarantee to meet the targets in all circumstances).

**337**  In terms of the general characteristic of service agreements, schools appeared to favour:

- annual agreements, with flexibility to vary arrangements mid year if needs changed;

- discounts for bulk purchase of services;

– basing the agreement on the academic rather than the financial year (this gives schools a longer period to make decisions on buy back once they have received notification of their budgets – it was also supported by several SLSs);

– allowing individual teachers to take out membership even if the school as a whole declined to buy back (this applied particularly to budget holders in secondary schools, eg heads of department).

**338**   In contrast, SLSs appeared to favour:

– agreements of more than one year. However, very few SLSs seem to have achieved this and some felt that the risk of predicting inflation and buy back levels in the future made the exercise hazardous, particularly as schools may expect a discount for signing a longer-term contract;

– inflation adjustment clauses in agreements of more than one year;

– at least one term's notice of termination of the agreement or the intention not to renew. However, this was proving difficult to enforce given the late notification of budgets to schools in many LAs.

**339**   Some SLSs also favoured the withdrawal of existing books on loan from school libraries where schools did not subscribe, in order to maintain the size of the SLS's overall bookstock. However, this was seen as a potentially insensitive move which could antagonise LA schools and sour relationships with the Education Department generally (for this reason it was deemed unacceptable by some LAs). Likewise, there were doubts about the legality of acting in this way against GM schools, where the book stock in the school at the time of incorporation as a GM school could be judged to be part of the school's property unless a prior agreement on ownership had been reached.

**Conclusions**

**340**   We conclude that service agreements should have the following characteristics:

– be written in clear, unambiguous plain English;

– be as concise as possible (this can mean covering only the main services in the agreement and leaving the various additional services to be covered by separate arrangements);

– set out the school's entitlement to service standards in terms of quantity, frequency and quality;

– set out the charges and the methods and times of payment;

– set out the period of time covered by the agreement;

– set out any penalties to be incurred by the SLS for not meeting agreed standards;

– set out the responsibilities of the school and the penalties for any loss or damage;

– describe the mechanisms for dealing with complaints.

**341**   In terms of the length of agreements we think agreements should be allowed to run until such time as the school (or the LA) decides to terminate the arrangement. Notice of a term should be required for termination. This would reduce the amount of effort which is currently expended on remarketing services to all schools annually, without reducing the ability of schools to withdraw from agreements when they wished. There would also be nothing to stop schools agreeing fixed points at which they wished to review the service formally with the SLS. We recognise, however, that this approach could have implications for other LA services to schools and also for LA policy generally.

**342**    Service agreements to GM and independent schools need to be constructed and written as legally binding contracts, although not couched in unnecessary legal language (which can be off-putting for schools).

**343**    Withdrawal of book stock from the school libraries of schools not subscribing to the SLS is, in our opinion, a legitimate action provided that schools have been given the opportunity to purchase their existing loan stock. This will be less contentious if it is made clear to schools prior to delegation that this is a necessary action to maintain the loan stock of the SLS. It is also easier if there are clear records showing which books in school libraries are the property of the SLS and which are the property of the school.

## Roles in the buying process

**344**    One of the characteristics of the SLS is that the main users are classroom teachers and their pupils, but decisions on purchasing are made by the senior management of the school, who may have less contact with the service. We therefore sought to explore the buying process and its implications.

### Findings

**345**    Many SLSs were keen to stress the wide differences between schools in how the buying process and decision making was organised. However, the following points emerged:

– **governors** appear to have more influence in primary than in secondary schools, and in GM than in LA schools. They were also more influential in the first year of delegation, after which they come to rely increasingly on advice from the headteacher. Teacher governors are seen as more accessible than other governors and as having more influence over buying decisions on curriculum related services. Governors can be useful in encouraging the school to have a long-term strategy towards buying services which avoids short-term decisions to opt in and out;

– **headteachers** are the main decision-makers in primary schools and often retain an interest and veto in secondary schools (although formal responsibility for purchasing decisions may be delegated to another senior member of staff). Headteachers may consider a decision on the SLS to be within their delegated authority (ie not requiring consultation with governors);

– **deputy headteachers** can have responsibility for budgeting matters in large primary schools and in secondary schools. This often means that purchasing decisions will be taken on their advice;

– **heads of departments** in secondary schools can be budget holders in their own right and an important influence on the school's purchasing decision. In some schools, funds for library purposes are 'top-sliced' from departmental subject allocations and then used to fund subscription to the SLS (as well as book purchase for the library within the school). Where budgets are delegated within schools, some SLSs have offered subscriptions to individual heads of department as well as to schools as a whole;

— **school librarians** or teachers-in-charge are seen as particularly influential, and many headteachers and deputy headteachers rely on their advice. A small number of SLSs expressed a fear that school librarians can have mixed motives when giving advice. Thus whilst most are very supportive of SLSs (in line with the policy of the School Library Association which represents many school and teacher librarians), examples were cited of cases where school librarians saw it as against their own interest (and even as a sign of personal weakness) to recommend continued use of the SLS;

— **teachers** are the main users of the service but are not budget holders and are not always consulted on decisions relating to the continued use of the SLS. However, in schools which do have a consultative approach to decision making (more often primary schools) they can be very influential;

— **school administrative officers/bursars** can be part of the decision making but usually defer to professional staff on curriculum related services. However, they are very receptive to value-for-money arguments;

— **parents** can have influence on decisions where they are organised through Parent Teacher Associations or through their representatives on governing bodies. They are likely to be most influential in primary schools where fund raising may augment library funds and book purchase and where volunteer parents often assist in maintaining the school library;

— **advisers/inspectors** can be influential. Advisers can affect school decisions through the advice they give – they are also customers in their own right through the LA's Advisory Service. Likewise, inspectors carrying out work for OFSTED will include inspection of the school library as part of a review of learning resources in the school generally. An OFSTED report highlighting inadequacies is likely to prompt action to improve matters.

**346**   Most SLSs have seen value in asking each school to nominate formally a 'school co-ordinator' for liaison/reporting purposes. The co-ordinator then becomes a source for identifying strengths and weaknesses of the service and the likelihood of future buy back. This approach can be supplemented by 'user groups' of teachers.

**Conclusions**

**347**   Each SLS needs to investigate and understand the general buying process in its own locality and, as far as possible, the specific process in individual schools (although we recognise that resource constraints mean that it is unlikely that SLSs can build up a complete picture of individual schools). The variety of arrangements means that a range of players need to be the targets of publicity and promotion activities. The aim should be to create a climate within and between schools which is conducive to them buying into the SLS.

**348**    Although the role of different players in the decision-making process is a matter for each school to decide, we would expect the influence of governors to decline over time as the LMS matures. This is because the use of educational support services by the school is likely to be interpreted as more an operational matter for professional staff than a strategic issue for governors.

**349**    In general SLSs should encourage decision-making processes by schools which allow the main users of services (ie teachers) to participate and make their views known. The promotion of school co-ordinators and user groups within schools, as well as representative forums across schools, should aid this process.

**350**    Schools should also be encouraged to take decisions collaboratively, or at least be aware of other schools' decisions and reasons. For example, some SLSs make sure that schools indicating their intention not to buy back in future are aware of the extent to which they are out of line with other schools; this may provoke them to reconsider their motives. Likewise, we know of LAs where schools informally canvas each other to see whether a general take up is likely – in one LA this extends to a meeting of headteachers where the impact of potential non-buy back by some is examined and collective decisions taken (although this does not bind individual governing bodies if they wish to dissent later). Of course, shared decision making by schools could also result in them deciding to opt out of a service *en masse* if that was the collective view.

## Value for money

**351**    Changes in decision-making processes in schools and improved service definition and marketing by SLSs will have little effect if schools do not consider services as good value for money. This is therefore a key issue for SLSs and one which many have highlighted as a priority.

**Findings**

**352**    The need to demonstrate value for money to schools has led to a variety of approaches from SLSs, many of which are used as part of their marketing effort. These include:

– quoting extracts from HMI reports and OFSTED inspections which stress the importance of school libraries and the necessity of adequate learning resources. Some SLSs thought a recommendation from OFSTED of a guideline spend per pupil on learning resources would be helpful, as well as research to show the link between learning resources and pupil performance;

– emphasising the savings to the school in time, stress and expense of teachers;

– highlighting the expertise of the SLS in terms of advice on book selection, meeting changing curriculum demands, and information selection and handling;

– displaying the breadth and quality of books and materials available through SLSs (eg through exhibitions);

– using 'value statements' for individual schools to show:
  – pre-delegation usage by the individual school;
  – the cost of continuing this level of usage post delegation through the SLS;

– the cost of doing so through book purchase.

This approach has the advantage of highlighting the level of previous use which is often underestimated by the school concerned. Similar 'value statements' can be provided on an annual basis post delegation;

– using 'value statements' in individual project/topic loan boxes. This has the advantage of demonstrating the value of items within the service and to the individual teacher;

– using HMI statements to emphasise the '£1 buys £9 through your SLS' message, sometimes customised by local experience;

– using personal testimonies from supportive headteachers and 'horror stories' from those who thought they could manage without the service for a period but now realise they cannot and have resumed their subscription;

– developing case study examples to show how good stock use can achieve school objectives at the fraction of the cost of alternatives;

– following up schools which make less than average use to determine the reasons;

– sending schools an itemised statement of service use (a bit like an itemised phone bill) with their bill so that the amount of usage is constantly emphasised. Charges expressed per pupil can also seem more reasonable than bare totals, particularly if delegation has used a per pupil formula;

– upgrading delivery and collection arrangements and the containers used (eg substituting plastic for cardboard boxes) to overcome a 'tatty but free' pre-delegation image;

– ensuring that service level standards are met, every time (this was seen as key by many SLSs – schools which once used the service sporadically now demand that the service agreement is met in full).

**353**   Several SLSs commented that, despite the changes the LMS has brought about, many schools remain confused about the concept of 'value for money' and how to assess it; thus making the task of satisfying the criterion more difficult. For some, the most important long-term strategy was to explore with each school individually how the SLS could help it meet its objectives and thus add value to the school's educational performance.

**Conclusions**

**354**   The attempts by SLSs to demonstrate value for money to schools fall into two main types:

– showing that use of the SLS raises standards of achievement and learning in schools;

– showing that use of the SLS is less costly than alternatives (eg book purchase).

**355**   Both are necessary but the former is more fundamental. For example, even if schools are convinced of the low cost of the service, they will not purchase it if they consider its contribution to achievement and learning is low. We are, therefore, attracted to approaches which work with schools to highlight the ways in which the use of the SLS helps them realise their educational objectives.

**356**  In terms of external assistance to make this case, we understand that OFSTED is unlikely to produce any supplement to the existing inspection handbook giving guidelines on spending on school libraries and learning materials. It will however, continue to emphasise the vital importance of these learning resources. OFSTED is also carrying out a major survey of school libraries and their impact on learning in schools (this is provisionally entitled *100 school libraries* and should be published in Autumn 1995).

**357**  Once the educational value of the service has been established and its cost compared with alternatives, considerations of efficiency come to the fore. This emphasises the importance of ensuring that service standards are met. We know from our experience in all service sector areas that customers penalise suppliers heavily for not hitting targets, even when the 'misses' are quite minor.

## Competition

**358**  Given that schools are free to use delegated budgets to purchase services from any provider we sought to establish the range of competitors which existed at present and those that might emerge in the near future.

### Findings

**359**  The main competition to SLSs comes from other demands on the school budget (eg extra teaching hours, provision for special educational needs) rather than from alternative providers of library services to schools. This confirms the view cited above that a fundamental task is for each SLS to convince schools that its service is value for money in meeting educational objectives, rather than just value for money against alternative providers.

**360**  In terms of the **loan** of books and materials there are no direct competitors for LA schools (other than the 'free' public library service discussed earlier). In GM and, to a lesser extent, independent schools, SLSs from other LAs were seen as potential future competitors (and real now in a few cases). Competition for loan services generally in the future was thought to be likely from other LAs' SLSs, subject to changes in restrictions on cross-border trading, although a few SLSs could foresee schools establishing their own consortium arrangements on a local basis.

**361**  We spoke to a number of commercial publishing organisations to assess the possibility of them entering the loan service market at some stage in the future. All confirmed that the need to establish a comprehensive loan stock and a network of outlets, together with the low profit margins in publishing generally, meant that it was extremely unlikely that any new commercial organisation would enter this market. In their view, any demise of the current SLSs would lead to a permanent decline in the loan service available to schools.

**362**  The same publishing organisations went on to emphasise the pivotal role that SLSs play in the publishing industry for children and young people. This is illustrated in *Figure 1* overleaf. SLSs act as a funnel for channelling the needs of schools to publishers and as a market and distribution network for publishers. Without the stability they provide, publishers indicated that the range of children's publishing would diminish significantly. In particular, without the guaranteed market that SLSs provide for the short print runs that are typical of this kind of publishing, publishers would concentrate more on material with a large potential market outside schools or outside the UK. For example, one speculated that material on the Vikings would still be published as it commands an international market, but material on, say, the Tudors and Stuarts might not as it would be reliant on sales to individual schools or parents in the UK.

**363** In terms of the **purchase** of books and materials by schools, competition is more real and diverse. The present supply chain of manufacturer (publisher), wholesaler (library supplier) and retailer (book seller, SLS) was seen as breaking down, with publishers, library suppliers and book sellers now all making direct approaches to schools. Competition in this area was thought likely to increase and some SLSs took the view that they should retreat from an overt selling role to providing independent advice to schools seeking to 'play the market'.

**364** The views of the publishing organisations to which we spoke were again of relevance. They emphasised the crucial role the SLS played in terms of introducing schools to new material (eg through organising visits to publishers and book previews) and advising schools on book purchase. Several noted recent examples of schools buying books direct from 'remainder' book sellers which, although heavily discounted, did not represent good quality or value for money. Some of the case study SLSs also expressed concern about the purchase of under-priced but out-of-date stock. The relative inexperience of many teachers and schools in buying books was highlighted both by publishers and SLSs.

**365** In terms of **advice and training** on library issues, competition was seen to exist from other LA units (notably the Advisory Service) and independent consultants (a burgeoning field of ex-LA and HMI inspectors, and chartered librarians). In some cases schools were also looking to their own internal resources (eg governors or parents with library skills) or to assistance from other schools (eg secondary school librarians giving advice to contributory primary schools). Again, this was seen as an area in which competition was likely to increase.

## Conclusions

**366** It seems unlikely that any commercial competition to provide a loan service to schools will emerge. Thus a decline of the SLS in any particular LA is likely to result in a permanent loss of this service to schools unless SLSs in other areas are able to intervene. Such a decline could have a negative impact on the delivery of the National Curriculum, particularly those aspects which depend on learning materials of the type currently provided through the project loan service to schools. Moreover, there is evidence to suggest that a general decline in SLSs would threaten not only the loan service to schools but also the range, quality and cost of some aspects of children's publishing.

**Figure 1**

# Structure of the children's publishing market for loan services to schools

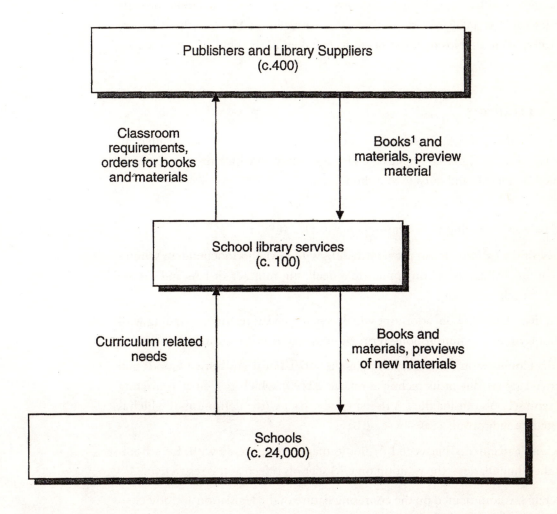

Note : 1 - Approximately 7,000 new titles and editions are published per annum

**367**   Competition in the areas of book purchase and advice and training is likely to increase. In order to enhance their competitiveness in these markets, SLSs should emphasise:

– their particular professional skills and attributes (eg matching curriculum needs to book selection, information search and handling skills);

– their independence from book sellers and publishers and their non-profit making nature;

– any important service enhancements they offer over competitors (eg book cataloguing).

**368**   Competition between different LA service units is wasteful of resources and needs to be governed by a corporate decision within the LA on who should provide which service (or how a collaborative service, say, between the SLS and the Advisory Service is to be offered). This decision needs to be taken in the light of school views.

## Barriers to trading

**369**   SLSs, as part of the LA, are subject to the restrictions on trading which affect all local authority services. This has implications for the extent to which they can provide services to schools inside and outside their home LA.

### Findings

**370**   The barriers to trading with schools perceived by SLSs are:

– the policy of the LA which can prevent trading with GM and independent schools locally (although this restriction applies in a declining number of LAs and can be expected to decline further);

– section 295 of the 1993 Education Act which is perceived as restricting trading with GM schools in the medium to long term (after a two-year 'breathing space' ends);

– the Audit Commission's interpretation of the 1970 Local Authority Goods and Services Act (as set out in its technical release 23/90) which is seen as restricting trading with schools outside the LA to marginal capacity (the definition of which is interpreted by auditors on a case-by-case basis);

– 'gentlemen's agreements' between LAs not to market to, or trade with, LA schools outside their boundaries – the position on GM schools is seen as less restrictive.

**371**   Several SLSs commented on the confusing nature of the legislation and advice so far received from various sources.

**372**   Those SLSs with a high and growing number of GM schools found the implications of the 1993 Act most threatening with several indicating that such a restriction might cause the service to fold or require it to investigate other possibilities (eg externalisation from the LA). Clarification of this aspect the 1993 Education Act from the DFE was awaited.

**373**   The restrictions on cross-border trading generally seemed less pressing. Few services appeared to be looking to expand significantly outside their home base in the short or medium term, with several pointing to the difficulties in meeting the extra demand even if all restrictions were lifted and they were successful in attracting wider business. However, some predicted the erosion of the 'gentlemen's agreement' between LAs on trading with LA schools or even its collapse.

**Conclusions**

**374**   We think that the possible implications of the 1993 Act for SLSs are more serious than other legislation on trading. This is because the high customer base required for viability of the SLS could be undermined by restrictions on trading with local GM schools. The relevant section of the legislation is set out in *Appendix F.*

**375**   We understand that the DFE is currently preparing a letter of advice and guidance on the application of this legislation that it will issue shortly. We believe that this will be of value not only to LA services but also to GM schools, many of which wish to continue to make use of LA support services such as the SLS.

**376**   The restrictions on cross-border trading appear less immediate but they too could threaten the viability of some SLSs by locking them into a declining market of schools in their 'home' LA.

# IV   Structure and management

## Introduction

**401**   In this section we consider issues relating to the structure and management of SLSs in the new trading environment. This includes the managerial freedoms required by service managers; management information and systems; trading structures and business planning; new business skills; relationships with other parts of the LA externalisation; and the impact of local government reorganisation.

## Managerial freedoms

### Findings

**402**   There are large differences in managerial freedoms between SLSs. For some the move to delegation has not been accompanied by any extra freedoms for managers, much to their disappointment. For others, the move has been accompanied by a wide range of changes such that managers do not feel the need for extra freedoms. These freedoms can be separated into the strategic and the operational.

**403**   The **strategic** freedoms relate to the ability of the service to choose what range of services it wishes to offer and to which customers. LAs generally find it easier to concede freedom over the service range than the customer base. This is because to allow service managers to choose which customers they wish to serve would impinge on wider areas of policy (eg towards GM or independent schools, or schools in other LAs, or types of schools within the home LA).

**404**   The **operational** freedoms sought are more easily conceded by LAs and relate to how services are developed and delivered. These relate mainly to finance, staffing and service delivery and can be summarised as follows:

- **financial freedoms:**
  - carry forward of surpluses and agreed deficits (in order to fund new developments and investment/replacement);
  - virement between budget headings without prior authority;
  - freedom from LA claw back during the financial year;
  - operation as a separate cost centre showing all costs, with a separate trading account for income and expenditure;
  - ability to make payments more promptly than central LA systems (eg via a cheque book and separate account);
  - ability to negotiate with central corporate departments and the public library service on support services and charges;

- **staffing freedoms:**
  - ability to determine staffing levels and grades;
  - ability to make short-term appointments;
  - ability to develop flexible pay systems and working practices, within any national or local agreements;

- **service delivery:**
  - ability to negotiate and deal with schools direct rather than always through the Education Department;
  - freedom to develop own separate publicity/promotional materials;
  - freedom to make contact and negotiate with outside agencies and sponsors.

**405**   The analogy with the freedoms of an LMS school were used by several SLSs as the appropriate model for the future.

### Conclusions

**406**   While some SLSs have sufficient managerial freedom, others clearly do not. We think that for as long as services are part of the LA then the LA must retain the right to set the framework and prescribe managerial freedoms. These are more likely to be prescribed in the strategic areas than the operational areas. Given that so many of the operational freedoms listed above have been granted to some SLSs, we see no reason why they cannot be extended to others; we recommend LAs to do so and think that this will enhance the viability of many SLSs. The financial freedoms would appear to be the most urgent.

## Management information and systems

**407**   Delegated budgets and effective management at the business unit rather than the LA level generally requires more detailed and accurate management information than existed previously. This is particularly true of the SLS which has a large customer base and diverse stock.

### Findings

**408**   Most SLSs appear to be still part of a pre-delegation management information system, typically designed for the needs of the public library service and the LA corporately. This is generally recognised as inadequate for operating as a trading unit in a more commercially orientated environment and some SLSs have developed (or are developing) bespoke systems.

**409**   There appears to be three main requirements:

- **stock management, including:**
  - database of all books and materials;
  - book ordering (preferably linked to suppliers);
  - recording of school orders and issuing receipts;
  - stock performance reports;

- **finance/accountancy, including:**
  - issuing of statements and invoices to customers;
  - production of trading accounts;
  - production of budget monitoring reports and analyses for managers;
  - time recording systems for staff;
- **customer service database including:**
  - entitlement and take up by customers (by school and by individual teacher), including usage-to-date reports;
  - information on school characteristics and status;
  - INSET records (by school and for groups of teachers in respect of the individual schools which they represent).

**410**   Some SLSs would also like information on the use of the public library service by teachers from different schools, copies of school and library development plans, and early sight of consultation documents on curriculum changes.

## Conclusions

**411**   SLSs will increasingly need more sophisticated management information systems based around a fully computerised library system, with stock control and financial management/accounting facilities. This may be available through in-house corporate developments. We suggest that individual SLSs should draw up a list of their perceived information requirements (sometimes called a Statement of User Requirements) in order to ascertain whether corporate developments will be adequate to meet their needs or whether stand-alone bespoke systems will be required.

**412**   Non-delegated SLSs should seek to tackle these information and systems requirements prior to delegation. This will allow more informed decisions to be made in the transition to trading, as well as releasing time for other management activities.

# Trading structures and business planning

**413**   The transition to trading for LA services has introduced a wide range of changes to organisational structures and planning processes, most of them imported from the commercial world.

## Findings

**414**   There is consensus amongst SLSs that they need to operate as separate cost centres with full trading accounts, regardless of the SLS's location in the departmental structure of the LA. The cost centre should capture all central administrative charges and support costs and display their breakdown (even though they are not open to negotiation currently in most LAs).

**415**   Most delegated SLSs have also found it vital to prepare a business plan, although the time available for doing this and the support available from other parts of the LA has varied widely. Experience indicates that at least six months is required to prepare an adequate business plan and that a participative approach to its production, involving as many staff as possible, is essential.

**416**    The relatively short-term contracts with schools and the annual budgeting cycle of the LA has meant that most business plans have been annual, with SLSs finding it difficult to project further ahead. Services which were established as cost centres and prepared their first business plans well before delegation, appear to have found the transition into delegation easier.

**417**    Several SLSs have moved to flatter management structures in an effort to reduce management overheads and increase efficiency. Some have also introduced new posts focusing on customer services, marketing, finance and quality assurance. At least one of the larger SLSs has restructured itself into separate sector-based teams (for primary, secondary, and special/nursery) to align itself more closely with its prime customer markets.

### Conclusions

**418**    The cost centre with trading account is the most appropriate structure for SLSs within the LA. Flatter management structures and the identification of new areas of responsibilities (eg finance, marketing) have also been a feature of many changes.

**419**    Business planning exercises need a minimum of six months' elapsed time and benefit from external support (from other parts of the LA if possible). Business plans should aim to project forward for more than one year, even though service agreements and budgets are annual. They should be reviewed annually although there may be a need to reconsider them more frequently if circumstances change dramatically.

**420**    The extension of the time horizon of business plans beyond one year should be seen as part of a process of raising more strategic questions about the direction of the SLS. It also prevents an entirely reactive stance to circumstances and allows the financial and staffing implications of future changes to be mapped out more precisely. Projections for three years ahead are desirable with best estimates for service take up, income and expenditure in years 2 and 3 (based on the extension of existing trends where no better information is available.)

**421**    A generic summary of business planning is included as *Appendix G*.

## New business skills

**422**    Operating in a more commercial fashion requires new business skills by service providers. These can have a profound effect on the culture of the service.

### Findings

**423**    SLSs identified a wide range of new skills that they felt were now required. These are summarised below:

– marketing, selling and negotiation;

– finance (including pricing, cost control, financial monitoring, accountancy);

– personnel management;

- enhanced IT and administrative skills;

- commercial stock control (eg practices such as 'Just In Time');

- business planning and strategic management;

- customer care;

- research and development;

- quality assurance.

The main new skills emphasised were finance and marketing/selling.

**424**    The effect of the movement to trading on the culture of the service was generally seen as profound. Most SLSs fear that a commercial ethos may come to supplant the traditional professional ethos of public service. The business jargon of the new approach make many staff uneasy and sentiments such as 'we are no longer librarians' were commonly expressed. However, SLSs still felt strongly that the leadership of the service should remain a professional librarian's post.

**425**    Many SLSs have responded to delegation with considerable commitment and energy, whatever misgivings they may have about the changes generally. There is also a small minority of SLSs which view the changes more positively and see the pursuit of a customer orientated approach as not in conflict with the previous service orientation, indeed even as a better method of fulfilling the old service orientation.

**Conclusions**

**426**    There is a range of new business skills required by SLSs if they are to develop successfully. The most prominent of these concern finance and marketing but this does not mean that services need to be run by accountants or salespersons, or that all staff need to be proficient in these skills. Many SLS librarians have already demonstrated the aptitude to acquire and develop these skills but LAs should identify and make provision to meet the new training needs of SLS staff.

**427**    A challenge for SLSs is to ensure that these new skills and the business ethos serve rather than supplant the best elements of the long-standing ethos of the service. In many respects this should be easier for SLSs than for many other educational services facing delegation, as SLSs have always had a strong customer orientation (in terms of a well-defined set of services and users, and a tradition of responsiveness to users' demands).

# Relationships with other parts of the local authority

**428**    The SLS has three main relationships with other parts of the LA: with other education units and the Education Department; with central support services; and with the public library service.

**Findings**

**429**    The relationship with other **education units and the Education Department** has become the most crucial for many SLSs. Given that most SLSs are located outside the Education Department, it is not surprising that the staff in many SLSs have felt a sense of isolation from other education services. This still exists in some cases but in most LAs relations appear to be closer than they were pre-delegation, with many SLSs reporting adequate involvement in planning and joint activities.

**430**    Strong formal and informal links between the SLS and other educational services trading with schools have produced close working relationships, as evidenced in joint marketing exercises and a pooling of information on schools. Mutual support in presenting a case to the corporate centre of the LA for changes in operating practices and procedures has also been beneficial. This close association is generally seen as preferable to open competition between units, even though the overlap between some aspects of services is recognised (eg advice and training on library issues by SLSs and by Advisory Services).

**431**    The relationship with the **central support services** (eg Chief Executives', Treasurers', Personnel, Property Services) has also been clarified as a result of delegation, although this is more of an issue for SLSs where there is little central holdback and these overheads costs must be passed on in charges to schools. In such cases there is greater need for SLSs to enter into service agreements with central departments in order to exercise some control over central costs and to ensure that support services meet requirements. This process is in its infancy inside most LAs but can be expected to grow as the service agreement culture spreads.

**432**    The relationship with the **public library service** is perhaps the most complex. The effect of delegation appears to have initiated a trend for SLSs to operate more independently of the public library service in which most are based. This has confirmed the wisdom of being outside the public library service in the eyes of the small minority of SLSs that are located in the Education Department.

**433**    However, a number of SLSs have made the counter-argument that the changes require the SLS and public library service to work more closely together. They also argue that location within the public library service helps protect and safeguard the SLS, particularly during the early years of delegation. This view is most strongly felt by those SLSs which look to greater integration in service delivery to schools by the public library service and the SLS in the future.

**Conclusions**

**434**    Close links and collaboration between the educational trading units (and other trading units perhaps) are more productive than open competition.

**435**    Central support services (and costs) should be increasingly under the control of trading units, such as the SLS, via service agreements.

**436**    The SLS and the public library service are likely to become more distinct in operational and service terms in most LAs. However, a number of shared support services are likely to remain and there is also a significant minority of SLSs where a differing philosophy and approach may lead to greater integration.

# Externalisation

**437**    In a small minority of LAs, some educational support services (but no SLSs to date) have been put at arms length from the authority, a larger number are considering the possibility. We refer to this as 'externalisation' which we prefer as a term to 'privatisation' as it encompasses organisational forms other than private companies.

**Findings**

**438**   There is little general enthusiasm amongst SLSs to be externalised from the LA. There is also no direct experience to draw upon although a few SLSs have looked into the possibility of trust status.

**439**   The advantages of such an 'externalisation' are seen as the freedoms that SLSs would have to trade freely and to make decisions independently of any LA structures or procedures. SLSs might also be able to escape high central support service costs, although some think that the need to find external support services might prove even more expensive.

**440**   The disadvantages of such a move are seen as a loss of security and continuity and of kinship with other education and public services (including the loss of professional contact, support and resources from the public library service). It was also seen as a further weakening of the professional ethos of the SLS, perhaps leading to a fundamental loss of identity. Some SLSs were not sure whether schools would understand the move or regard the service so favourably after the change.

**441**   A major stumbling block to externalisation was seen as the high transfer cost of the book stock which it was assumed that the new venture would need to purchase (at market rates) from the LA. It was not clear who would finance this significant initial investment.

**442**   Despite these reservations, many SLSs regarded their externalisation from the LA as inevitable in the long term, with some seeing it as part of government policy.

**Conclusions**

**443**   The advantages of externalisation are not clear to SLSs and most view it in negative terms. However, given that many SLSs view it as inevitable it demands serious consideration. In *Appendix H* we set out some of the forms it might take and their possible advantages and disadvantages.

## Local government reorganisation

**444**   The possible ramifications of the Local Government Review is preoccupying most services in County LAs. We considered it from the perspective of the SLS but we were aware that this was only a small part of the debate about library services and education services generally.

**Findings**

**445**   The implications of the break up County LAs were almost universally seen as very threatening by the SLSs within them and likely to result in a fragmented and diminished service. A loss of economies of scale, specialist expertise and breadth of service was predicted, with rural areas (where costs tend to be higher) suffering most from any reorganisation. No counter-vailing advantages for unitary authorities were cited.

**446**   SLSs identified three main options:

– the service is 'externalised' from the LA prior to abolition, either alone or in association with other services, and is then funded partly by schools and partly by the successor LAs (who may also have representation on the board of the new body);

– the service is inherited in whole by one of the successor LAs which runs it on behalf of the other new LAs and forms a committee with them to oversee the service on a consortium basis. This is seen as attractive in principle but (given the experience of the break up of the Inner London Education Authority) difficult to sustain beyond the early period in practice. There are also issues connected with the legal basis of any such arrangement;

– the service is divided up into smaller separate services which are run by the successor LAs. This is seen as costly and likely to result in a much diminished service (if any at all in some areas given that the SLS is not a statutory service and a few existing LAs manage without one).

**447**   Local government reorganisation is also perceived by some SLSs as likely to presage a steep increase in the number of schools seeking GM status. This will in itself push SLSs into more of an open trading relationship with schools regardless of whether the existing or successor LAs have this as a policy objective.

**448**   Metropolitan LAs are not affected directly but largely share this pessimistic view. A few see opportunities to expand out from metropolitan areas into parts of surrounding County areas if cross–border trading restrictions are relaxed.

**Conclusions**

**449**   Local government reorganisation is likely to have a major impact on the SLS in County areas. If current arrangements are fragmented the likelihood of this being to the detriment of services and schools is strong, with a consequent loss of economies of scale, specialist expertise and breadth of service. There are alternatives to fragmentation but these involve, as yet, untried consortia or externalisation approaches and are not without their potential disadvantages.

**450**   In our view, SLSs which have experienced delegation and have a track record of trading with schools are more likely to survive the changes brought about by reorganisation, whatever organisational form they take.

# V  Conclusion

**501**  The summary prefacing the report sets out the main conclusions of the review. This final section does not repeat the points made there but instead provides a concluding overview.

**502**  The SLS has traditionally played a key role in ensuring a cost-effective and high-quality supply of learning materials to the vast majority of maintained schools in England and Wales. The importance of this role has been reinforced by the introduction of the National Curriculum which has resulted, *inter alia*, in a significant growth in the scope and quantity of project-related materials required by schools.

**503**  The concurrent trend towards delegation of budgets to schools has been less marked for the SLS than for some other learning support services. However, there is evidence to suggest that SLSs are not able to adapt easily to the sharp changes in demand for services that can result from budget delegation, particularly when this is accompanied by actual reductions in school budgets overall. These difficulties may cause some LAs to decide against delegation.

**504**  We believe, nevertheless, that the traditional SLS, if it is of high quality and valued by schools, can survive and succeed under a delegated system. However, the pace and nature of that delegation needs to be carefully considered in order to take account of some of the characteristics of SLSs. In particular delegation should only be introduced after an adequate period of planning and preparation and in full consultation with schools.

**505**  The rapid change which is now a feature of the educational world is likely to continue, and may indeed accelerate with the prospect of further changes arising from the Local Government Review. It is therefore important to continue to monitor the state of health of SLS provision to schools. This is particularly the case as no alternative service to schools currently exists or appears likely to emerge in the short term. There are also wider implications for children's publishing as a whole, should the SLS in general suffer a marked decline.

## Appendix A

# Detailed list of issues considered by the review

The following issues, framed as questions, were agreed by the Steering Committee at the start of the review. They were sent to all SLSs in England and Wales and written submissions were invited.

## Resource allocation and delegation

- What are the advantages and disadvantages of a centrally funded service as opposed to a delegated service?
- What are the most advantageous methods of allocating resources for delegated services through the LMS formula?
- What should be the timing of delegation and what are the advantages and disadvantages of different phasing arrangements?
- What impact is delegation likely to have on public library systems in terms of services to children (eg stock provision by public libraries, access rights by teachers and children, relationships between school library and public library services) and of support services (eg bibliographical or technical and IT support), and how might any adverse effects be overcome?
- What are the problems of disentangling school library budgets from the budgets for other library services and how can these problems be overcome?

## Marketing of services

- What should be the relationship between the costs of providing services to schools and the charges made for them, and how might this need to change over time?
- How can the markets for services be defined and what market research techniques have proved successful?
- How can the service 'offer' be defined (eg through the use of 'packages' of services) and what have proved the best ways of informing schools of the 'offer' to be made available to them?
- How can potential new services which schools might buy be identified and what promotional activities have proved successful?
- What are the characteristics of service agreements which both meet the needs of schools and the requirements for future service viability (including those elements of agreements which schools find most and least attractive)?
- What are the different roles within the buying process (eg of head teachers, governors, heads of department, members of staff responsible for the library) and what impact do these roles have on the likelihood of schools continuing to purchase services?
- How can services best demonstrate value for money to schools?

– What is the range of existing competitors and what future range is likely to emerge?

– What are the barriers to services trading with schools locally (eg constraints in relation to GM schools) and with schools in other LAs, and what impact might these have?

## Structure and management

– What freedoms do service managers need within the local authority in order to respond swiftly to the demands of schools and to manage their services effectively?

– What changes in management information and systems are necessary for effective management?

– What trading structures and business-planning processes are appropriate, and what are the best timescales for their implementation?

– What range of new business skills do service providers need to develop and what is their potential effect on the culture of services?

– What are the most appropriate relationships with other business units and parts of the local authority?

– What are the merits of more arms length arrangements, either inside or outside the local authority (eg business units, trusts, companies)?

– What are the implications of local government reorganisation and the prospect of smaller unitary authorities in many areas?

## Appendix B

# Responses to invitation to provide written submissions

## Submissions from LAs

Avon
Barnsley
Bedfordshire
Berkshire
Bexley
Birmingham
Bolton
Bradford
Brent
Bromley
Buckinghamshire
Cambridgeshire
Camden
City of London
Coventry
Croydon
Cumbria
Dorset
Dyfed
Ealing
East Sussex
Enfield
Essex
Gloucestershire
Gwent
Gwynedd
Hampshire
Haringey
Harrow
Havering
Hereford &
    Worcester
Hertfordshire
Hounslow
Islington
Kent
Knowsley
Lancashire
Leeds

Leicestershire
Liverpool
Mid Glamorgan
Newcastle
Norfolk
North Tyneside
North Yorkshire
Northamptonshire
Northumberland
Nottinghamshire
Powys
Redbridge
Rotherham
Salford
Shropshire
Solihull
Somerset
St Helens
Stockport
Suffolk
Surrey
Sutton
Tameside
Wakefield
Walsall
Wandsworth
Warwickshire
West Glamorgan
Westminster
Wigan
Wirral
Wolverhampton

## Submissions from National Bodies

Association of Metropolitan
    Authorities
Committee of Welsh Services
Library Association

## Publishers and publishing organisations contacted

Askews Library Supplies
Educational Publishers
    Council
Franklin Watts
Wayland Publishers Ltd

## Appendix C

# Summary of characteristics of case studies

| | Level of delegation | Formula allocation | Service offer/charges | Level of buy back of schools (1994/95) | Management |
|---|---|---|---|---|---|
| Cheshire | Delegation to secondary schools | Lump sum and per pupil element (including weighting for social needs) | 3 levels of service for secondaries, standard charge per level. Extra services charged at cost | secondary – 92% | Separate cost centre within Information and Leisure Services. Service agreement to Education |
| Devon | Devolution to all schools | Allocation to each school equal to precise cost of buying back service for school of that size and type | Single package. Schools also offered discount on book purchase | all schools – 98% | Head of the SLS in Education Department, rest of staff in public library service |
| Hillingdon | 50% delegation to all schools | Lump sum, covering a number of curriculum support services | 3 packages for primary with charges per pupil. 4 for special, charges per package. Secondary offer is based on 3 modules, charges per module | primary – 97% secondary – 60% special – 100% | Part of Local Services Group which includes public library service. Separate cost centre |
| Kirklees | Not delegated | – | Statement of service aims for all schools but no formal service agreements | – | Located in Cultural Services Department. Not a separate cost centre. Includes museums loan service |
| Lincolnshire | 85% delegated to primary and secondary schools | Age Weighted Pupil Unit | Single package, varying in school size. Charges per pupil | all schools – 82% | Service unit in public library service. Agency agreement with Education Department |
| Sandwell | 92% delegated to primary and secondary schools | Age Weighted Pupil Unit | Single package, for primary and for secondary. Charges per package. Pay as you use available as more expensive option | primaries – 72% secondary – 58 special – 82% (all schools – 71%) | Within Leisure Department, Libraries, Heritage and Arts Division. Not a separate cost centre |

## Cheshire education library service

### Background

Cheshire LA is a County Council with 64 secondary schools, 464 primary schools and 23 special schools. There are also 3 secondary and 3 primary GM schools.

The Cheshire ELS budget is approximately £900,000. The staffing complement is 14.8 posts (6 professional, 8.8 administrative).

### Level of delegation

The ELS has been delegated to secondary schools since April 1993. It is not delegated to primary or special schools.

### Formula allocations

The ELS budget is allocated via a lump sum and per pupil element. The per pupil element also contains a small weighting (+15%) for pupils in receipt of free school meals.

### Service offer/charges

Secondary schools are offered three levels of subscription for loan items with a fixed charge for each level. Other services are offered on a pay-as-you-use basis, mainly for consultancy and advice. All schools receive a free initial consultancy service with charges for any subsequent in-depth work.

Bespoke packages for any mix of services are available on request.

GM schools are charged 5% extra to cover central charges.

### Level of buy back

In 1993/94, 95% of secondary schools bought back (all LA schools, but none of the GM schools). This has fallen slightly to 92% of secondary schools in 1994/95.

Although not delegated to primary, the one GM primary that existed at the time chose not to buy back the service offered in 1993/94. The two new GM primary schools are buying back in 1994/95.

### Management

The ELS is part of the Information and Leisure Services Department and operates under a service level agreement with the Education Department. It is a separate cost centre. The LA operates on internal market for support services.

## Devon schools library service

### Background

Devon LA is a County Council with 57 secondary schools, 441 primary schools and 21 special schools. In addition there are 6 secondary and 1 primary GM schools.

The Devon SLS has a budget of approximately £1.15m per annum. The staffing complement is 26.8 full-time equivalent (FTE) divided between a Headquarters and four areas. HQ consists of a head of service and a co-ordinator, the areas comprise in total 8 professional staff, 1 advisory teacher, 4 centre managers and 11.8 support staff.

## Level of delegation

The SLS is not delegated to schools. Instead 90% of the budget has been devolved to schools from April 1993, with 10% retained to cover non-school services provided. The SLS is one of 12 support and advice services devolved in this way such that schools have an earmarked sum that must be spent on these services. It is possible to vire funds between the devolved services but not to use the devolved budget to buy non-devolved services, nor to use the school's delegated budgets to buy more of the devolved services. The funds for devolved services are held as a discretionary exception within the LMS scheme.

## Level of buy back

In 1993/94, 99% of schools bought back the service offered. This has dropped slightly to 98% in 1994/95.

Schools are encouraged to take their decisions on support services collectively within clusters and networks.

## Formula allocation

80% of the SLS budget was allocated to primary schools and 20% to secondary schools. Within each sector the allocation to each school reflects the cost of that service to the school were it to opt to purchase it.

## Services offered/charges

The SLS offers a basic package to all schools that comprises:

– book loan service with fixed number of exchanges;

– topic loan service, available on demand;

– subsidised book purchase scheme (at a discount originally made possible by a separate annual subsidy from the Education Committee and now built into the devolved budgets);

– book ordering;

– professional support on library issues.

In addition a number of new optional extra services are being offered for the first time in 1994/95:

– fiction collections aimed at pupils at key stages 2 and 3;

– book selections to support pupils with reading difficulties;

– computerised cataloguing systems for schools;

– pre- and post-OFSTED advice.

Charges are based on a fixed sum per school plus a per pupil element. Charges to GM schools are higher to recover a proportion of central costs.

## Management

The head of the SLS is within the Education Department and is a member of both the Education Department and Library Services management teams. The other members of staff are part of the public library service.

It is organised on an area basis with four areas.

# Hillingdon schools library service

## Background

Hillingdon LA is an outer London borough in West London with 3 secondary schools, 59 primary schools and 6 special schools. In addition there are 12 secondary and 11 primary GM schools.

Hillingdon SLS has a budget of approximately £150,000 per annum. This supports a staff of 4.9 FTE (2 FT professional, 1 FT administrative, 2 PT staff and seasonal support).

## Level of delegation

The SLS has been delegated to primary and secondary schools since April 1992 and to special schools since April 1993. Only 50% of funds are delegated. The balance is held as a discretionary exception to cover all costs except salaries (ie central overheads and the book stock).

## Formula allocation

The LMS formula contains a lump sum 'curriculum protection factor' to cover the SLS and some other educational support services. The notional allocation for the SLS is not identified.

## Service offer/charges

There are seven elements to offer to primary and secondary schools:

– project box service;

– fiction loan service;

– artifact collection of different faiths and cultures;

– teacher resource ticket for SLS library;

– fiction and poetry boxes;

– purchase assistance service;

– consultancy advice.

Primary schools are offered three options: a standard package of all seven elements, similar to that provided pre-delegation; and two packages which vary the project box service against the fiction loan service. Charges are at a standard rate per pupil. GM charges are twice that of LA schools to reflect the LA level of central holdback.

Special schools are offered an additional option to primary schools. Charges for each of the four options are at a fixed package price.

Secondary schools are offered three modules with a number of options within them:

– Module A is the project box loan service, with a minimum level and a series of levels above this;

– Module B is the fiction loan service, for which three levels are offered;

– Module C is a package of the five other services offered.

Charges are per module, with a discount for schools buying all three modules.

## Level of buy back

| | Percentage of schools buying back | | |
| --- | --- | --- | --- |
| | 1992/93 | 1993/94 | 1994/95 |
| primary | 100 | 100 | 97 |
| secondary | 88 | 53 | 60 |
| special | – | 100 | 100 |

### Management

The SLS was part of the Education and Community Services Department until 1993. It is now part of a 'Local Services Group' which includes the public library service to which it reports. The retained parts of its budget are funded by the Education Committee.

The SLS was established as a separate cost centre in 1987. Three annual business plans have been produced since delegation.

# Kirklees education library service

### Background

Kirklees LA is a metropolitan borough council in West Yorkshire with 23 secondary schools, 7 middle schools, 162 primary schools and 9 special schools. There are also 2 GM secondary schools.

The budget for the SLS is approximately £180,000 per annum. The staffing complement is 10.6 (7.5 professional, 3.1 administrative).

### Level of delegation

The service is not delegated to schools. This follows two consultation exercises with schools in 1992 and 1993 which both indicated large majorities in favour of central retention.

### Formula allocation

Not relevant. However, schools are allocated an entitlement to some services (eg book loans) and receive information on their use of the service against this entitlement.

### Service offer/charges

The services offered consist of the following elements:

– fiction and non-fiction book loan up to a fixed entitlement per pupil;

– project loans of multi-media resource;

– advisory services and INSET;

– publications;

– artifacts and object loans.

INSET activities are charged to schools at the LA's average daily cost for general INSET (which is higher than SLS costs), Schools are also charged for some publications.

**Level of buy back**
Not relevant.

**Management**
The Kirklees SLS is known as 'Books +' and combines a service to schools with a museum service. It is also responsible for the children's books sections of the public library service.

The SLS is part of the Cultural Services Department with the cost of the service charged to the Education Committee budget.

# Lincolnshire schools library service

**Background**
Lincolnshire LA is a County Council with 46 secondary schools, 284 primary schools and 19 special schools. In addition there are 22 secondary and 15 primary GM schools.

The Lincolnshire SLS has a budget of approximately £350,000 per annum. The staffing complement consists of 4.75 professional staff, 9 library assistants/drivers operating the mobile libraries and managing the stock, and 1 part-time assistant.

**Management**
The SLS is part of the Department of Recreational Services and managed by the Principal Librarian, Special Services, whose responsibilities also cover library services for elderly people in residential homes. It was restructured in 1989 to allow it to function separately from the children's library services of the public library service. Detailed guidelines setting out the different functions of the SLS and the public library service have been drawn up and sent to public libraries.

**Level of delegation**
The SLS has been delegated to all primary and secondary schools since April 1991. 85% of the budget was delegated and 15% held back for marketing, central administration and management.

Delegation was extended to special schools in April 1993. This leaves only nursery schools outside delegation.

**Formula allocation**
10% of the budget was allocated to secondary schools and 90% to primary schools.

**Level of buy back**
In 1991/92, 92% of schools bought back the service, falling slightly to 90% in 1992/93. In 1993/94 and 1994/95, 82% of schools bought back the service.

**Service offer/charges**
The SLS offers a single package for schools, without any options. The package consists of the following elements:

– a book loan service with mobile library visits once a term for primary schools and twice a year for secondary schools;

– curriculum support packs;

- loan of sound recordings;

- professional advice on the school library;

- book purchase from the mobile library;

- organised visits to a library supplier.

The package varies between primary and secondary schools only in terms of the volume of the entitlement to different elements.

Charges are per pupil and are higher for primary schools than secondary schools (reflecting the greater usage of the service by primary schools).

## Sandwell education library service

### Background
Sandwell LA is a metropolitan borough in the West Midlands with 19 secondary schools, 112 primary schools and 11 special schools. There is also one GM secondary school.

Sandwell ELS has a budget of approximately £120,000 per annum. The staffing complement is 4 (3 professional, 1 administrative).

### Level of delegation
The ELS has been delegated to primary and secondary schools since April 1992 and to special schools since April 1994. 92% of the budget is delegated, with 8% for central overheads.

### Formula allocation
The ELS budget was added to the Aggregated Schools Budget and allocated via the general formula (ie mainly by Age Weighted Pupil Units). This resulted in 40% of the budget being allocated to the primary schools and 60% to the secondary schools (previous service usage was estimated to be 10% secondary and 90% primary).

### Management
The ELS is within the Department of Leisure, Libraries, Heritage and Arts Division. ELS is part of Youth and Education Services (YES) which provides a combined service to schools and children's service to the public library service.

The head of YES is charged 50% to the ELS and 50% to the public library service.

### Level of buy back
100% of primary schools bought back in 1992/3, 89% in 1993/4 and 72% in 1994/5. 80% of secondary schools bought back in 1992/3, 53% in 1993/4 and 58% in 1994/5. 82% of special schools bought back in 1994/95.

### Service offer/charges
Schools are offered a fixed annual subscription package or a 'pay-as-you-use' approach.

The subscription package for primary schools consists of a core unit supplemented by one of four levels of the project fiction loan service (depending on school size). The core unit consists of:

- short-term loans for teachers from the Exhibition collection;

– video loans;

– loans from the Teachers' Professional Libraries Collection;

– use of Exhibition collection to assist book purchase;

– one copy of all ELS publications;

– one advisory visit on request.

Charges are per school, with four levels of charge to reflect different school sizes.

Secondary schools are offered a single package similar to the primary schools but without any variations for school size. There is a fixed package charge.

Any school can opt for 'pay as you use' as an alternative to a package although charges are higher (*pro rata*). Schools subscribing to a package can also use 'pay as you use' to buy extra services at a cheaper rate than non-subscribing schools.

# Steering Committee and consultancy team

## Steering Committee for review

| | |
|---|---|
| Lesley Blundell | Department of National Heritage |
| John Tucker | Department for Education |
| Stewart Robertson | Office for Standards in Education |
| John Burchell | British Library Research and Development Department |
| Catherine Blanshard | Assistant Director, Hertfordshire Libraries |
| Yvonne Gill-Martin | Assistant Chief Librarian, Bolton |
| Linda Hopkins | County Librarian, Gloucestershire |

## Coopers & Lybrand Consultancy Team

| | |
|---|---|
| Quentin Thompson | Director |
| John Lakin | Manager |
| Peter Howlett | Consultant |
| Mike Nichol | Consultant |

## Appendix E

# New services and service variations highlighted in written submissions and case studies

## New services

- pre-OFSTED advice on writing/reviewing a school library development plan and reviewing school library provision (this includes monitoring published OFSTED reports and sending schools extracts so that they are aware of OFSTED concerns);

- post-OFSTED advice on writing and implementing a school library action plan;

- loan service for works of Art (pictures/sculptures) via an Art Club and separate subscription. Emphasis on modern and multi-cultural art produced by local students and artists;

- INSET programme for teachers focusing on development planning, policy framing and information search/handling skills;

- new research packs based more closely on National Curriculum;

- advice on maximising the learning potential of CD ROM and other new technologies;

- greater involvement in advice on assessment of pupils.

## Service variations

- revised fiction loan service targeted at junior-age pupils (to offset previous bias towards infant-age pupils);

- reduction of number of books in loan boxes to make service cheaper to schools;

- introduction of pre-packed loan boxes (but later withdrawn because of difficulty of tailoring boxes to exact year groups and problems of slow return of items from schools).

# Legislation on trading with GM schools

## Education (Schools Act) 1993

Section 295 – (1) Where the Secretary of State by order provides for this section to apply to a local education authority, the functions of the authority shall include the supply by the authority of such goods or service as may be specified in the order to the governing bodies of grant-maintained or grant-maintained special schools in such area as may be so specified.

(2) The area specified in the order may not extend beyond the area which comprises:

(a) the area of the authority; and

(b) the area of any other local education authority which shares any boundary with the authority.

(3) The terms on which goods and services are supplied by a local education authority in the exercise of a function exercisable by virtue of this section shall be such as can reasonably be expected to secure that the full cost of exercising the function is recovered by the authority.

(4) This section may not apply to a local education authority after the expiry of the period of two years beginning when it first applies to the authority.

(5) This section is without prejudice to the generality of any other enactment conferring functions on local education authorities.

## Appendix G

# Summary of business planning

## Introduction

**1**   Most SLSs, faced with delegation, have drawn up a formal business plan to assist the transition to a trading position. Often this has been required by the LA and supported by advice and guidance from officers in central departments. This appendix sets out some general points about business planning which may be of use to SLSs about to go through this process or to those reviewing their earlier experiences.

## What is a business plan?

**2**   There is no single definition of a business plan or the process by which one should be produced. Instead, a reasonable consensus exists on the types of issue the plan should cover and the range of approaches that can be used in the business planning process. This makes business planning more an art than a science. SLSs should consult within their authorities, in order to see whether a standard approach to business planning exists. If so, this should be followed unless there is good reason not to, as the audience for the plan within the authority will be familiar with the approach, as will officers who are required to contribute to the plan (eg finance officers for cost breakdowns).

**3**   For SLSs in authorities without a preferred approach, a business plan can be defined as a written statement of the actions and resources required by an organisation to sustain and develop its activities over time. Looked at another way, it is a method of asking and answering a series of key questions about an organisation:

– Who are we?

– What do we do and what do we want to do?

– Who are our customers and what do they want?

– Who are our competitors and what are they doing?

– What should we do next and what will it cost?

**4**   Business plans can have various audiences but the main one for the SLS should be the managers and staff of the service itself. The wider LA obviously has a clear interest too and senior officers outside the SLS will undoubtedly need to approve the final plan.

## Common elements of a business plan

**5**   Although the order and the emphasis may vary, a business plan should expect to contain the following items:

– a summary of the background and context to the service (who are we?);

– a review of the current position or status (where are we?);

- a statement of the strategic aims and objectives of the service (where do we want to go?);

- an action plan showing the actions required and resource requirements (how do we get there?);

We consider each section in more detail.

## Background and context

**6** This section should summarise the context for the service and the business plan. It might set out details of the location of the service within the authority's structure, list the services it offers and the budget it controls, and state the main factors (legislation, technology, market pressures) which are likely to cause change. This should be a short factual section taking up no more than 10% of the document.

## Status review

**7** The purpose of this section is to review the needs of customers and the strengths and weaknesses of the organisation in meeting them (including competition with any competitors). It normally consists of an internal assessment of the organisation (in terms of structure, people, culture, systems, costs and services) and an external assessment of the market(s) (in terms of customers, suppliers, legislation, competition and funding).

**8** These two aspects are often brought together in a SWOT analysis which analyses the strengths and weaknesses of the organisation against the opportunities and threats which exist. This section of the plan might be expected to constitute 30-40% of the document.

## Strategic aims and objectives

**9** The purpose of this section is to identify the strategic way forward for the service so that an action plan can be developed. It should include an expression of the purpose (or mission) of the service and the core values it intends to uphold. These may be informed by wider statements made by the LA, or they may need to be generated from first principles by the service itself. They should, however, be 'owned' by managers and staff as far as possible and not be imposed from above.

**10** This section should also include an outline of the services to be provided to achieve these objectives. This should define the service, the methods of delivery, the volume and costs, and the charges to be made. The section in total might comprise around 30% of the plan.

## Action plan

**11** The final section should identify clearly what needs to be done, who will do it, how and when it should be done, and how success (or failure) will be measured. It will also need to show the resources required to carry out the actions in terms of money, people, systems, buildings and equipment. There should be a performance measure (or indicator) for each activity or outcome specified. This section of the plan might comprise 20-30% of the document.

# The business planning process

**12** It has become commonplace to say that the process of producing a business plan is as important as the final document itself. This is because the plan is only as good as the commitment and enthusiasm generated to carry it out. If the process is seen as merely a paper exercise then a poor plan is likely to result.

**13** These considerations mean that a team approach is normally used over a period to draw up the plan, consulting with a wider group at intervals. For small services it should be possible to include all members of staff in these wider consultations. The team leading the process and drafting the plan will necessarily be smaller, however, and may be chosen to be representative of the wider service (in specialism and/or grade); it should be led by a senior manager of the service.

**14** The process should involve assessing customer views at some stage. This can be through market research already available but often requires new research with customers to be carried out (through interviews or surveys).

**15** The activities required to produce the plan must be planned and managed. The entire process is unlikely to take less than three months the first time around and may take as long as six months.

**16** As a possible checklist to aid planning the following ten steps might be useful:

– Step 1 – select the core business planning team.

– Step 2 – decide how to consult and communicate with other staff throughout the process.

– Step 3 – decide format of plan.

– Step 4 – set timescales for development and approval of the plan.

– Step 5 – allocate responsibilities.

– Step 6 – allocate resources.

– Step 7 – develop plan (using the four sections outlined above if appropriate).

– Section 8 – review output/amend plan.

– Section 9 – secure political, corporate and staff commitment.

– Step 10 – start implementation.

### Review and update

**17** Business plans are normally updated annually. This should be a much less time-consuming process than production of the first plan but it should share some of the same characteristics, such as consultation with staff.

**18** Although plans are reviewed annually it is helpful if they cover more than a single year. The normal projection periods are for three to five years, although three years is probably adequate for the SLS. Actions should thus be scheduled over three years and services and costs projected over the same period. The level of detail in years 2 and 3 will obviously be much less and should be guestimates where the figures are not available (as will normally be the case). The excuse that annual budgeting procedures or the high level of future uncertainty makes it impossible to look more than a year ahead should be avoided.

**19** A useful analogy is that with an artist completing a landscape: the foreground represents year 1, inked in and firm; the middle distance represents year 2, sketched in but subject to change; the far distance represents year 3, pencilled in lightly and likely to be revised considerably. Each year when the plan is rolled forward year 2 is inked in to become the new year 1, year 3 is sketched in more firmly to become the new year 2, and a new year 3 is pencilled in for the first time.

## Common difficulties

**20** The most common difficulties experienced when producing a first business plan are:

- **Time pressures** – business planning asks difficult questions which need time and resources to be answered. However it is best to see the process as integral to managing the service rather than as an extra duty to be carried out.

- **Lack of information** – this most frequently relates to cost data not being broken down sufficiently or in the right format. Some accountancy support here can be invaluable but the business planning process should not be seen as a finance driven exercise.

- **Cynicism** – managers and staff may see it as a paper exercise of no real value. Commitment from senior management may help here plus the development of a process which involves staff and demonstrates that they are the prime audience/beneficiary of the exercise.

- **Inexperience in forecasting changes/risks** – this can be overcome by looking at a range of possible variations rather than a single prediction. Worst case/best case scenarios can be useful, particularly if the different implications for each can be shown.

# Forms of externalisation

**1**   This appendix identifies the principal alternative organisational options which exist for externalisation of LA services such as the SLS. In assessing these, there are three key considerations to be addressed:

– legal status;

– charitable status and trading;

– control and influence.

## Legal status

**2**   There are a limited number of types of legal status for new organisations. Those generally considered applicable are:

– a trust;

– an Industrial and Provident Society;

– a limited company, limited either by guarantees or by shares.

**3**   The detail of each of these legal forms is explained below.

### Trust

**4**   This is the traditional legal form for endowed, grant-giving charities and for charitable fund-raising bodies. They are usually registered under the Charities Act 1960 and operate under a trust deed as self-perpetuating bodies run by designated trustees.

**5**   A trust does not normally have a large membership. However, it is possible for the trust deed to allow for the establishment of a membership group, which may have its function defined as fund raising and establishing public support for the trust. These members would not be responsible for running the trust, although one or more trustees might be chosen from their number.

**6**   It is possible for the trust deed to state the 'constituencies' from which trustees are to be drawn, thus reserving some places for representatives of different bodies and interest groups (eg the local authority, residents and users, and staff).

**7**   A trust is reasonably straightforward to set up and run. Trusts are almost always charities and as such are answerable to the Charity Commissioners, submitting annual accounts to them.

### Industrial and Provident Society

**8**   Industrial and Provident Societies are corporate bodies registered under the Industrial and Provident Societies Act 1965. To qualify for registration, a body must be a bona fide co-operative or a society established for the benefit of the community. It usually adopts model rules to assist registration. This is a common type of legal status for housing, consumer and worker co-operatives, for credit unions and for housing associations, provided they do not make distributable profits.

## Limited Company

**9**   Limited companies are corporate bodies registered under the Companies Act 1985. There are three main types of company:

– a public limited company (plc), which may issue shares to the public (eg: British Gas, high street banks etc). Such companies are usually large capital-based ventures and trade for the purpose of making a profit;

– a private limited company, which restricts the issue of shares to selected individuals, and distributes any profit to its shareholders. A company limited by shares is unable to register as a charity;

– a private company limited by guarantee whereby each member guarantees a certain sum (which may be a nominal sum such as £1) in the event of the company being wound up. This is a common form of incorporation for charities, and is acceptable to the Charity Commission if it meets certain criteria.

**10**   The general advantages and disadvantages of each of these legal forms of externalisation for LA services are summarised overleaf in *Figure 2*. However, it is important to stress that these need to be examined in more detail and in the light of local conditions before a definite decision can be made about the most appropriate form for any individual service.

## Charitable status and trading

**11**   A trading body is one which exchanges goods or services for profit, either for private gain or to benefit the community. Charities, on the other hand, are community benefit organisations which have, as their objects, one of the particular activities recognised in British law as being charitable. A charitable trust is required to register with the Charity Commission. Industrial and Provident Societies and companies limited by guarantee can also have charitable rules whereby their profits are not distributed.

**12**   A charity must have purposes which the law regards as exclusively charitable. There are four purposes or 'heads' accepted in law:

– the relief of poverty;

– the advancement of education;

– the advancement of religion;

– other purposes beneficial to the community not falling under any of the other heads.

*Figure 2:* **General advantages and disadvantages of different legal forms of externalisation for LA services**

| Legal status | Advantages | Disadvantages |
|---|---|---|
| Trust | – local authority nominees can form majority or all of trustees without prejudice<br>– accounting and reporting requirements are simple<br>– recognised as reputable and trustworthy<br>– good public image<br>– can have charitable status | – Trustees have unlimited personal liability<br>– Organisational framework inflexible and unlikely to promote commercial management disciplines<br>– has to await Charity Commission registration (which can take up to one year) before it can operate |
| Industrial and Provident Society | – limited liability<br>– can apply to Inland Revenue for treatment as a charity<br>– simple accounting and reporting requirements<br>– can have charitable status | – registration expensive and slow unless model rules used<br>– model rules limit scope of Society to housing and related activities<br>– unlikely to be familiar to the public, employees or some funding institutions |
| Company limited by guarantee | – limited liability<br>– the word 'limited' can be dropped to enhance public image<br>– familiar status to public, funding institutions and employees<br>– flexible and commercial orientation<br>– can apply for charitable status but can operate whilst awaiting registration | – complex Companies Act reporting requirements<br>– must use commercial accounting procedures |
| Company limited by shares | – limited liability<br>– familiar status to public, funding institutions and employees<br>– commercial and flexible orientation<br>– ease of raising capital from funding institutions | – complex Companies Act reporting requirements<br>– must use commercial accounting procedures<br>– profit distribution to shareholders<br>– cannot be charitable body<br>– may have public image problem to schools |

**13** Although it is a matter for the Charity Commissioners, and it has not been tested through an application, it seems likely that the Schools Library Service would be accepted as having a charitable purpose under the head for the advancement of education. A charity is run by trustees (sometimes referred to as governors, committee members or directors) who are responsible for its affairs but who may appoint paid staff to carry out the day-to-day management.

**14** Certain activities are specifically defined as not charitable. These include:

– certain political, campaigning and pressure group activities;

– permanent trading;

– arrangements where the persons running the organisation benefit personally.

**15**   Trustees have to accept some personal liability for the affairs of a charity – the exact extent of this will depend on the legal structure of the charity.

**16**   It is not necessary for all charities to register with the Charity Commissioners to gain the benefits of charitable status. Those not required to register include:

– some very small charities;

– societies registered under the Industrial and Provident Societies Act 1965.

**17**   A charity can sell its services if this matches its fundamental purpose as detailed in its rules or articles. For example, if the fundamental purpose of a charity is stated as the housing of elderly people, then the charity can charge for services relating to that. Similarly, a charity registered for the purpose of teaching music could charge for that function and may also carry out any incidental trading, such as selling sheet music to pupils. It is, however, unlikely that it would be permitted to sell instruments from a shop to the general public since this would be judged as permanent trading and therefore non-charitable.

**18**   If any significant trading is anticipated, then a model in which a wholly owned subsidiary is used to protect the charitable status of the recent body is often used. A company limited by guarantee or trust is established with charitable status; this carries out the fundamental purpose of the charity (eg teaching music). A wholly owned subsidiary is then set up, which is normally a company limited by guarantee but without charitable status. The subsidiary carries out any trading activities (eg selling instruments to the public) with any profits covenanted back to the parent body (and therefore tax exempt).

**19**   It is important to note that although the two bodies must maintain separate accounts, they can operate closely together (eg share the same senior management, registered office etc).

**20**   Charitable status carries a number of significant advantages:

– exemption from corporation tax and stamp duty;

– public image benefits;

– access to sources of financial support available only to charities;

– tax concessions for donors;

– proposed exemption from Local Government and Housing Act 1989 controls;

– ability to make a surplus;

– exemption from Business Rates.

**21**   However it must be borne in mind that a charity:

– cannot reclaim VAT (although partial exemption for certain trading activities may be allowable);

– must provide an element of public benefit;

– is non profit distributing.

# Control and influence

**22**    The Local Government and Housing Act 1989 defined forms of companies (including Industrial and Provident Societies) in which a local authority may have an interest. These are:

− controlled companies;

− influenced companies;

− other minority interest companies.

## Controlled Companies

**23**    A 'controlled company' is defined as one in which a local authority owns more than half the shares or controls more than half the votes at a general meeting or on the Board of Directors. A controlled company has majority board representation by the local authority and would be subject to:

− capital finance controls (ie any borrowing or related arrangements entered into by the company would count against the authority's capital limits);

− trading activities might not be permitted (this is discussed more fully below);

− a full range of procedural and administrative constraints would apply, much as they currently do to the local authority itself.

**24**    Whilst the 1989 Act itself came into effect on 1 April 1990, the regulations required to effect the detailed controls have not yet been issued by the Department of the Environment. Currently there is still no firm indication of when these may be available. There are, therefore, considerable uncertainties, about the precise form of controls and whether they will apply retrospectively. It is prudent, however, to assume that these controls will be implemented eventually.

**25**    The legislative framework is founded on the Government's view that companies which local authorities control, by means of a majority interest on the board, should form part of the local authority sector for financial control purposes and should be bound by similar propriety and procedural standards. In this regard, there is no intention to distinguish between companies which authorities themselves seek to establish and companies which they are required to establish (for example, airport companies, transport undertakings and, more recently, waste disposal companies).

## Influenced Companies

**26**    Less restrictive controls are intended to apply to companies which are defined as 'influenced'. An influenced company is one where the local authority board representation is between 20% and 50% and where half or more of the company's turnover derives from business with the local authority. It should be noted that it is possible for influenced charitable companies which can demonstrate genuine independence from the authority to be exempted from legislative controls, but this proposed exemption does not extend to charitable controlled companies. An influenced company would be free to trade outside of local authority restrictions but is likely to be inside local authority capital controls.

## Other Minority Interest

**27**   'Minority interest' companies are defined as companies where the local authority board representation is less than 20% or where less than 50% of the business is with the local authority. They are free of all the local authority trading or capital restrictions that apply to controlled or influenced companies.

## Joint Venture

**28**   All of the company forms, except those where local authority share ownership or board representation is total (ie 100%) or absent (ie 0%), can be referred to as joint ventures. A joint venture simply means that the shares of the company, or board representation, are split among one or more bodies.

Prepared for the Department of National Heritage and published October 1994.
Printed in the UK for HMSO. Dd298368 C8 10/94 3400 5673.